best of **ani difranco** for

# GUiTAR

Transcriptions by Steve Gorenberg, Colin Higgins, Jeff Jacobson, Matt Scharfglass and Jeff Story

ISBN 978-0-634-03223-3

**HAL•LEONARD®**
**CORPORATION**
7777 W. BLUEMOUND RD. P.O. BOX 13819 MILWAUKEE, WI 53213

Visit Hal Leonard Online at
**www.halleonard.com**

The book you hold in your hands has been a decade in the making. For years, people have been requesting the sheet music to Ani DiFranco's songs, and those of us who handle such requests at her record label have always been caught empty handed, with only a fan-based website of well-intentioned but unauthorized guitar tabs to recommend ... until now.

Thanks to the fine folks at Hal Leonard, most of Ani's albums starting with *Little Plastic Castle* currently have (or will eventually have) accompanying songbooks whose contents have been compiled and double-checked by a crack team consisting of Hal's Angels plus Reg Dickinson (Ani's tireless guitar tech and Keeper of the Tunings) and the Little Folksinger herself. "All very well and good," you say, "but what about the albums before that?"

Ani does indeed have 15 not-so-compact discs to her name at the moment I'm writing (and by the time this particular moment passes, she'll surely have released another 2 or 3), so it would take an entire rack in your local music store to house books for all of them. Which brings us to the present volume: Ani's hand-picked selection of 20 tunes as originally recorded on her solo albums through *Dilate* in 1996. Ani specifically chose the songs in this book with solo guitar in mind; a second *Best Of* collection focuses on arrangements for piano and guitar of 21 more songs from the solo albums through *Up Up Up Up Up Up* in 1999. You'll find material here dating all the way back to Ani's self-titled first album, released in 1990, including some longtime crowd-pleasers as well as songs she hasn't regularly played live in years. Brought together under a single roof, they provide an in-depth look at Ani's continual exploration of the sonic possibilities of the acoustic guitar and her well-documented history of alternate tunings. (Anticipating another couple of frequently asked questions, Ani's primary guitars for most of her career have been Alvarez-Yairi WY1s, and her much-noted homemade "claws" consist of press-on nails glued to her fingernails and fortified with electrical tape.)

So here they are: a highly personal compendium of 20 of Ani's best. Learn 'em, play 'em, enjoy 'em — and remember, there's plenty more where these came from.

RON EHMKE – RIGHTEOUS BABE RECORDS MINISTER OF COMMUNICATIONS

# CONTENTS

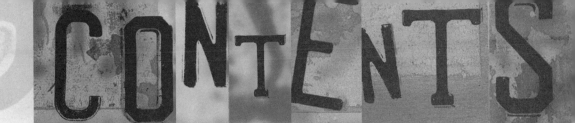

Ani DiFranco
**1990**

Well over a decade into her career, songwriter, guitarist, and vocalist Ani DiFranco has toured the globe countless times playing to ever-larger and louder audiences, many of whom appear to know every one of her lyrics by heart, including a few she herself has long forgotten. During that time, Ani has released a steady stream of self-produced solo recordings, a pair of collaborations with storyteller Utah Phillips, and numerous side projects on her own label, Righteous Babe Records. In short, she's a perpetually busy grrrl for whom the word "vacation" is simply not an operational concept.

Not So Soft
**1991**

**"DiFranco has an artistic infinity ahead of her, as her example continues to stimulate hope that not everything, and everyone, can be bought and sold."**

—THE [STOCKTON,CA] RECORD

Born in the Rust Belt mecca of Buffalo, New York in 1970, Ani's earliest exposure to music came not from pop radio, but from the folksingers who stayed overnight with her family while making their way across the Northeast. The intimacy and hand-to-mouth economics of the essentially underground folk tradition fueled Ani's own passion for live performance, and she began singing and playing acoustic guitar in Buffalo bars before she turned 10. By age 15, she was writing songs of her own, and soon she was hitting the coffeehouse and club circuit herself. By the time audience members encouraged her to record an album in 1990, Ani had more than 100 original compositions from which to choose: observations about life in her hometown, chronicles of social injustices, journal-like accounts of family dynamics and the politics of the heart. Like countless performers before and after her, Ani chose to release that first cassette herself, without waiting for a label to sign her. Borrowing money from friends, the 20-year-old produced her own self-titled debut album and sold it from the trunk of her car while blazing a trail across the seedy dives and (sometimes seedier) university campuses of North America.

Imperfectly
**1992**

Puddle Dive
**1993**

Like I Said
**1993**

Photo by SCOT FISHER

Out of Range
**1994**

Not a Pretty Girl
**1995**

Dilate
**1996**

Living In Clip
**1997**

Fourth-generation dubs of that tape and its successors sparked interest in Ani from coast to coast, along with ecstatic word of mouth, college and non-commercial radio airplay, and rapturous reviews in zines, college and city papers, and music magazines. Offers from labels large and small poured in, but unlike many young artists under similar circumstances, Ani decided to continue releasing albums herself, which allowed her a far greater degree of artistic freedom than any outside interest would have provided. For Ani, independence is and always has been a political act.

Everything happens organically in DiFranco-land. (As Ani puts it, the guiding principle is "Demand before supply.") Both the touring crew and the in-house staff have gradually grown in order to meet increasing need, and Ani's income from concerts, record sales, licensing arrangements, and merchandise is channeled directly back into future projects, which in turn allow her to support like-minded fellow artists, Buffalo businesses, and grassroots activists and culture workers. Perhaps the best example of this process is the appearance of albums recorded by other artists on Righteous Babe, starting with discs by Arto Lindsay, Sekou Sundiata, Sara Lee, and Kurt Swinghammer.

In an era when a handful of multinational corporations control 80% of the music industry, Ani is truly on her own and quite happy that way. In her steadfast refusal to compromise her own vision, Ani embodies, as a writer for the *St. Paul Pioneer Press* once put it, "the soul of a shaman, the courage of an activist, and the voice of a generation."

"...the best Ani DiFranco songs have a bell-like clarity that signals steadfast resistance to projections and expectations — it's the chiming of a sensibility that, while constantly changing, is never less than its own."

—SONICNET

you are subtle as a window pane
standing in my view
but i will wait for it to rain
so that i can see you
you call me up at night when there's
no light passing through
and you think that i don't understand
but i do

we don't say everything
that we could
so that we can say later
oh, you misunderstood
i hold my cards
up close to my chest
i say what i have to
and i hold back the rest

someone you don't know
is someone you don't know
get a firm grip, girl
before you let go
for every hand extended
another lies in wait
keep an eye on that one

**ANTiCiPATe**

anticipate
dress down and get out there
pick a fight with the police
we'll get it all on film
for the new release
seems like everyone's an actor
or they're an actor's best friend
i wonder what was wrong
to begin with
that they should all have to pretend
we lose sight of everything
when we have to keep
checking our backs
i think we should all just smile,
come clean and relax

but he says
someone you don't know
is someone you don't know
get a firm grip, girl
before you let go
for every hand extended
another lies in wait
keep an eye on that one
anticipate
if there's anything i've learned
all these years on my own
it's how to find my own way there
and how to find my own way
back home

from *Not So Soft*

# ANTICIPATE

**Words and Music by Ani DiFranco**

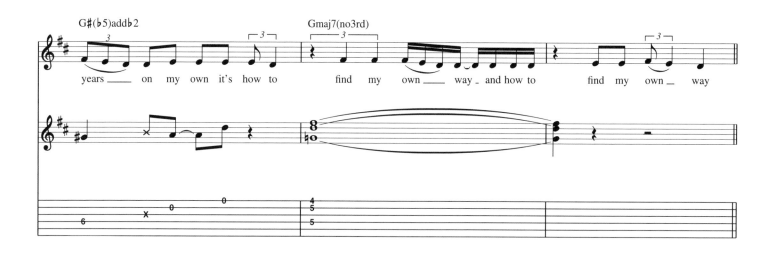

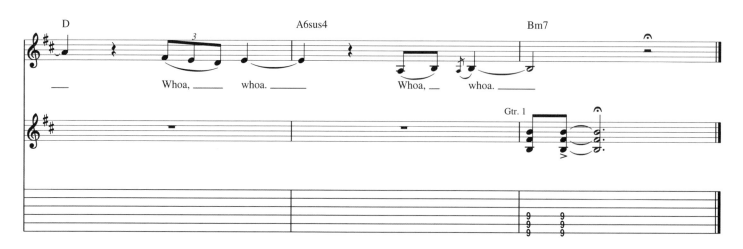

# BLOOD iN THE BOARDROOM

sitting in the boardroom

the i'm so bored room

listening to the suits

talk about their world

they can make straight lines out of almost anything

except for the line of my upper lip when it curls

dressed in my best greasy skin and squinty eyes

i'm the only part of summer that made it inside

in the air-conditioned building decorated with a corporate flair

i wonder can these boys smell me bleeding thru my underwear

there's men wearing the blood of the woman they love

there's white wearing the blood of the brown

but every woman learns how to bleed from the moon

and we bleed to renew life every time it's cut down

i got my vertebrae all stacked up high as they can go

but i still feel myself sliding from the earth that i know

so i excuse myself and leave the room

saying my period came early but it's not a minute too soon

i go and find the only other woman on the floor

it's the secretary sitting at the desk by the door

i ask her if she's got a tampon i can use

she says oh honey what a hassle for you sure i do you know i do

i say it ain't no hassle no it ain't no mess

right now it's the only power that i possess

these businessmen got the money

they got the instruments of death

but i can make life i can make breath

sitting in the boardroom

the i'm so bored room

listening to the suits talk about their world

i didn't really have much to say the whole time i was there

so i just left a big brown blood stain on their white chair

from *Puddle Dive*

# BLOOD IN THE BOARDROOM

**Words and Music by Ani DiFranco**

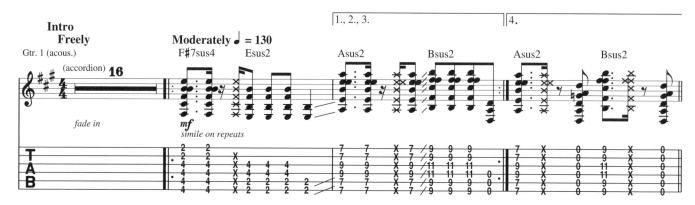

DADGAD Tuning:

① = D  ④ = D
② = A  ⑤ = A
③ = G  ⑥ = D

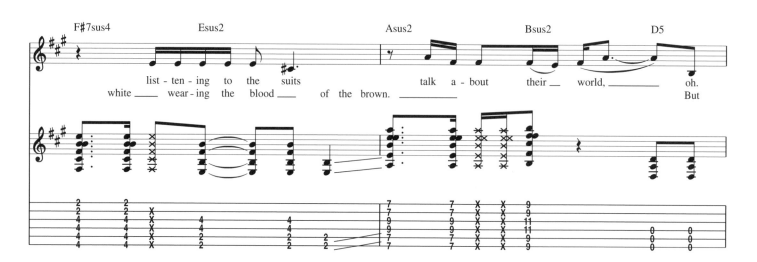

1. Sit - ting in the board - room, the I'm so bored room,
3. There's men wear - ing the blood of the wom-en they love; there's
5. *See Additional Lyrics*

list - en - ing to the suits talk a - bout their world, oh.
white wear - ing the blood of the brown. But

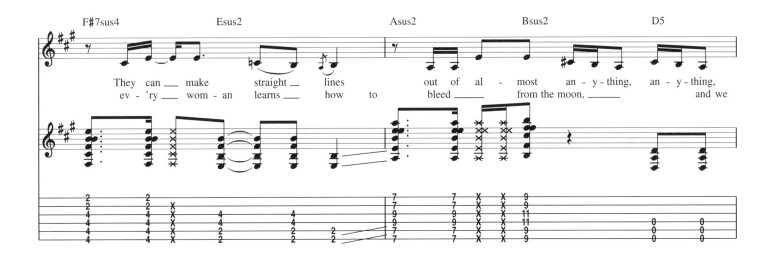

They can __ make straight __ lines out of al - most an - y - thing, an - y - thing,
ev - 'ry __ wom - an learns __ how to bleed _____ from the moon, _____ and we

ex - cept for the line __ of my up - per lip when it curls.
bleed _____ to re - new life ev - 'ry time it's cut down. __ 4. I got my

**End Rhy. Fig. 1**

## 𝄋 **Verse**

Gtr. 1: w/ Rhy. Fig. 1, simile

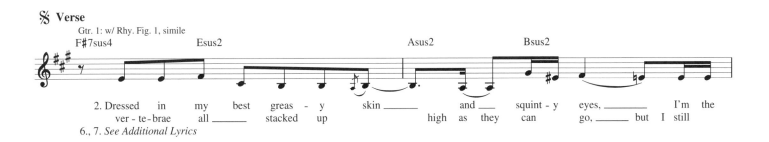

2. Dressed in my best greas - y skin _____ and __ squint - y eyes, _____ I'm the
ver - te - brae all _____ stacked up high as they can go, _____ but I still

6., 7. See Additional Lyrics

on - ly part of sum - mer here __ that made it in - side _____ in the
feel my - self slid - ing from the earth that I know. So I just

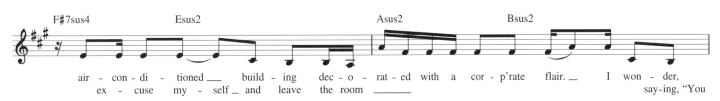

air - con - di - tioned __ build - ing dec - o - rat - ed with a cor - p'rate flair. __ I won - der,
ex - cuse my - self __ and leave the room _____ say - ing, "You

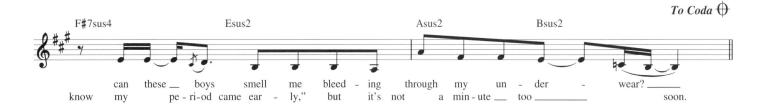

F#7sus4    Esus2    Asus2    Bsus2

can these \_\_ boys smell me bleed - ing through my un - der - wear? _____

know my pe - ri-od came ear - ly," but it's not a min - ute \_\_ too _____ soon.

**Interlude**

Gtr. 1
F#5    **Rhy. Fig. 2**    A5    E5    A5

*simile on repeats*

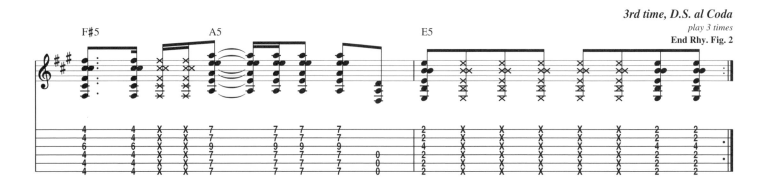

*3rd time, D.S. al Coda*
*play 3 times*
**End Rhy. Fig. 2**

F#5    A5    E5

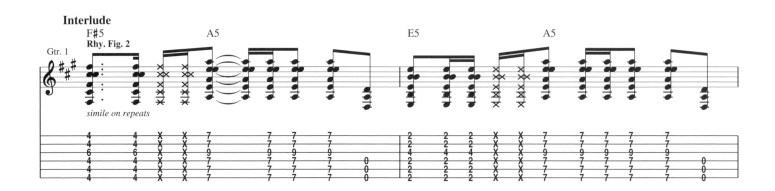

⊕ *Coda*

**Interlude**

Gtr. 1: w/ Rhy. Fig. 2, simile

4

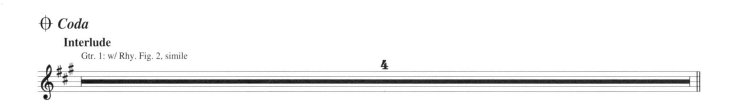

**Outro**

w/ Bkgd. Voc. ad lib., next 9 meas.    Gtr. 1 tacet
F#7sus4    N.C.

Sit - ting in the board - room, the I'm so bored room, lis - ten-ing to the suits

Gtr. 1

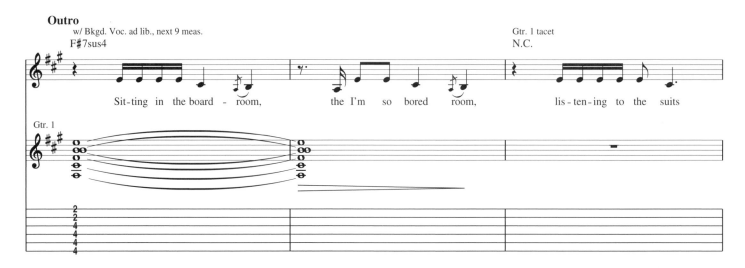

talk a-bout their world. _____ They can make a straight _ line out of al - most an - y-thing, an - y-thing.

*rit.*

They can make a straight _ line, they can make, they can, they can... Sit-ting in the board - room,

**Free Time**

the I'm so bored room. Sit-ting in the board - room, the I'm so bored room.

Sit-ting in the board - room, the I'm so bored _ room. Sit-ting in the sit-ting, sit-ting,

*Lead voc. gradually fades out over next 3 meas.

**Begin Fade** **Fade Out**

(accordion)

**5**

sit-ting in, sit-ting sit - ting... Sit-ting in the board - room.

*Additional Lyrics*

5. I go and find the only other woman on the floor;
   It's the secretary sitting at the desk by the door.
   I ask her if she's got a tampon I can use.
   She says, "Oh, honey, what a hassle for you.
   Sure, I do, you know I do."

6. I say, "It ain't no hassle, no, it ain't no mess."
   Right, right now it's the only power that I, that I possess.
   Those businessmen got the money.
   They got the instruments of death.
   You know, I can make life,
   You know, I can make breath.

7. Sitting in the board room,
   The I'm so bored room,
   Listening to the suits talk about their world.
   I didn't really have much to say,
   The whole time I was there.
   So I just left a big brown blood stain on their white chair.

buildings and bridges
are made to bend in the wind
to withstand the world
that's what it takes
all that steel and stone
are no match for the air my friend
what doesn't bend breaks
we are made to bleed
and scab and heal and bleed again
and turn every scar
into a joke
we are made to fight
and fuck and talk and fight again
and sit around and laugh
until we choke
i don't know who you were expecting
probably some bitch
who does not budge
with eyes the size of snow
i may get pissed off sometimes
but you seem like the type
to hold a grudge
and in the end i just let it go
buildings and bridges
are made to bend in the wind
to withstand the world
that's what it takes
all that steel and stone
are no match for the air my friend
what doesn't bend breaks

BUILDINGS
AND
BRIDGEs

from *Out of Range*

# BUILDINGS AND BRIDGES

**Words and Music by Ani DiFranco**

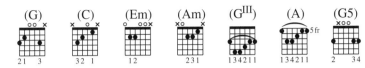

(G)   (C)   (Em)   (Am)   (G$^{III}$)   (A)   (G5)

Capo III

**Intro**
Moderately ♩ = 98

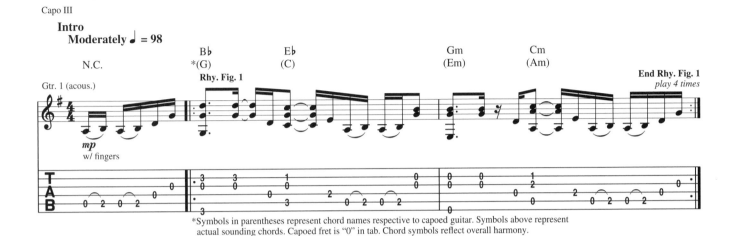

*Symbols in parentheses represent chord names respective to capoed guitar. Symbols above represent actual sounding chords. Capoed fret is "0" in tab. Chord symbols reflect overall harmony.

**%. Verse**

Gtr. 1: w/ Rhy. Fig. 1, 3 1/2 times, simile

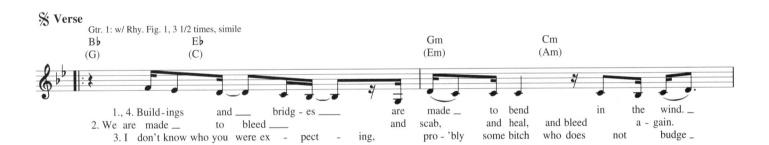

1., 4. Build-ings and __ bridg-es __ are made __ to bend __ in the wind. __
2. We are made __ to bleed __ and scab, and heal, and bleed a - gain.
3. I don't know who you were ex - pect - ing, pro - 'bly some bitch who does not budge __

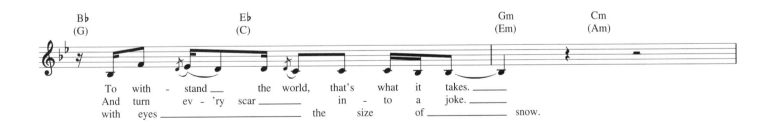

To with - stand __ the world, that's what it takes. __
And turn ev - 'ry scar __ in - to a joke. __
with eyes __ the size of __ snow.

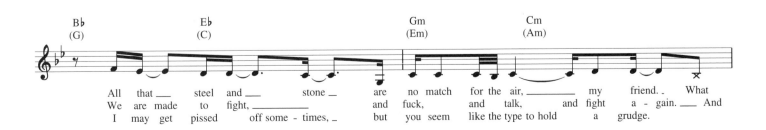

All that __ steel and __ stone __ are no match for the air, __ my friend. __ What
We are made to fight, __ and fuck, and talk, and fight a - gain. __ And
I may get pissed off some - times, __ but you seem like the type to hold a grudge.

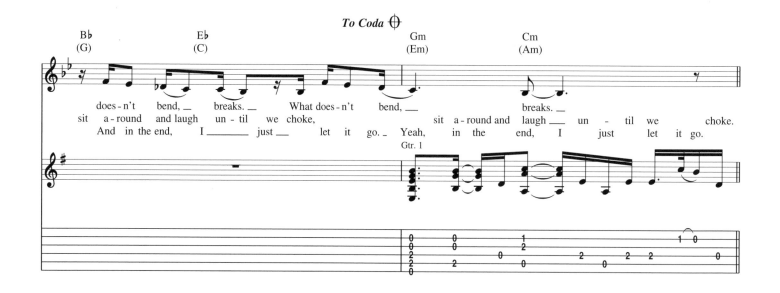

## Chorus

# DILATE

life used to be life-like
now it's more like show biz
i wake up in the night
and i don't know where the bathroom is
and i don't know what town i'm in
or what sky i am under
and i wake up in the darkness and i
don't have the will anymore to wonder
everyone has a skeleton
and a closet to keep it in
and you're mine
every song has a you
a you that the singer sings to
and you're it this time
baby, you're it this time

when i need to wipe my face
i use the back of my hand
and i like to take up space
just because i can
and i use my dress
to wipe up my drink
i care less and less
what people think
and you are so lame
you always disappoint me
it's kinda like our running joke
but it's really not funny
i just want you to live up to
the image of you i create
i see you and i'm so unsatisfied
i see you and i dilate

so i'll walk the plank
and i'll jump with a smile
if i'm gonna go down
i'm gonna do it with style
and you won't see me surrender
you won't hear me confess
'cuz you've left me with nothing
but i've worked with less
and i learn every room long enough
to make it to the door
and then i hear it click shut behind me
and every key works differently
i forget every time
and the forgetting defines me
that's what defines me

when i say you sucked my brain out
the english translation
is i am in love with you
and it is no fun
but i don't use words like love
'cuz words like that don't matter
but don't look so offended
you know, you should be flattered
i wake up in the night
in some big hotel bed
my hands grope for the light
my hands grope for my head
the world is my oyster
the road is my home
and i know that i'm better
off alone

from *Dilate*

# DILATE

**Words and Music by Ani DiFranco**

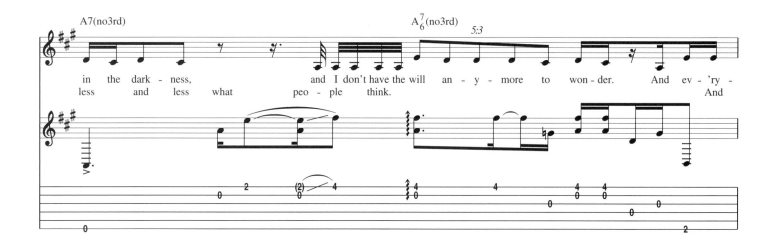

in the dark - ness, and I don't have the will an - y - more to won - der. And ev - 'ry -
less and less what peo - ple think. And

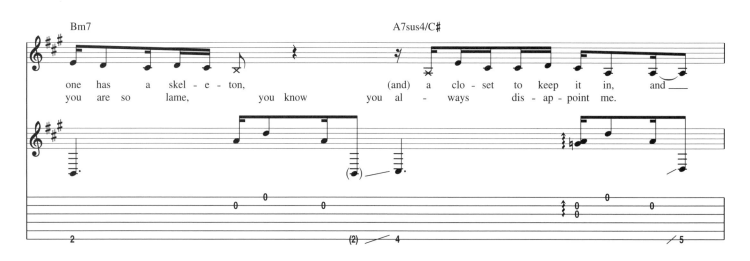

one has a skel - e - ton, (and) a clo - set to keep it in, and ___
you are so lame, you know you al - ways dis - ap - point me.

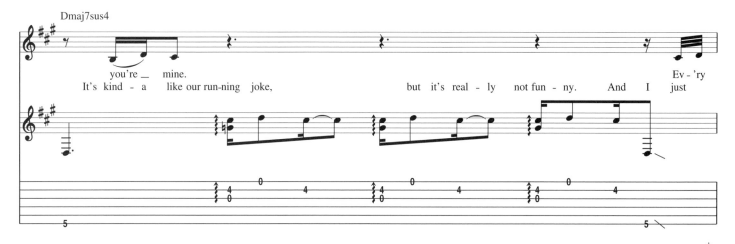

you're ___ mine.
It's kind - a like our run - ning joke, but it's real - ly not fun - ny. And I just

*To Coda 1* ⊕
*To Coda 2* ⊕

song has a you, a you that the sing - er sings to,
want you to live up to the im - age of you I cre - ate.

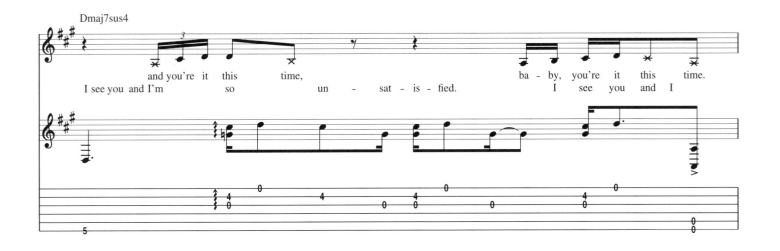

Dmaj7sus4

and you're it this time,
I see you and I'm so un - sat - is - fied.

ba - by, you're it this time.
I see you and I

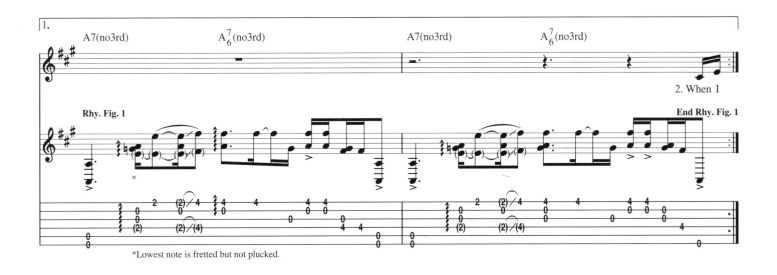

**1.**

A7(no3rd)    A⁷₆(no3rd)    A7(no3rd)    A⁷₆(no3rd)

2. When I

Rhy. Fig. 1

End Rhy. Fig. 1

*Lowest note is fretted but not plucked.

**2.**

Gtr. 1: w/ Rhy. Fig. 1, 2 times, simile

*D.S. al Coda 1*

A7(no3rd)    A⁷₆(no3rd)    A7(no3rd)    A⁷₆(no3rd) A7(no3rd) A⁷₆(no3rd)    A7(no3rd)    A⁷₆(no3rd)

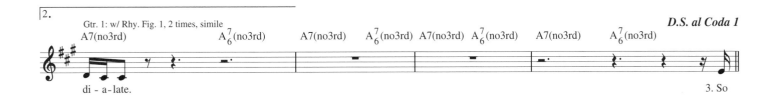

di - a - late.

3. So

⊕ *Coda 1*

Dmaj7sus4

**Chorus**
A7(no3rd)    A⁷₆(no3rd)
Voc. Fig. 1

for - get - ting de - fines ___ me,    yeah, that's what de - fines ___ me.
Oh,    ho,    ho. ___

Rhy. Fig. 2

## Coda 2

### Additional Lyrics

3. So I'll walk the plank,
   And I'll jump with a smile.
   If I'm gonna go down,
   I'm gonna do it with style.
   And you won't see me surrender,
   You won't hear me confess
   'Cuz you've left me with nothing
   But I've worked with less.
   And I learn every room long enough
   To make it to the door
   And then I hear it click shut behind me;
   And every key works differently
   And I forget every time,
   And the forgetting defines me,
   Yeah, that's what defines me.

4. And when I say you sucked my brain out,
   The English translation
   Is I am in love with you
   And it is no fun.
   But I don't use words like love,
   'Cuz words like that don't matter.
   But don't look so offended;
   You know, you should be flattered.
   And I wake up in the night
   In some big hotel bed;
   My hands grope for the light,
   My hands grope for my head.
   And the world is my oyster, you know,
   The road is my home
   And I know that I'm better,
   I'm better, I'm better
   Off alone.

# THE DINER

i'm calling from the diner
the diner on the corner
i ordered two coffees
one is for you
i was hoping you'd join me
'cause i ain't got no money
and i really miss you
i should mention that too

yes i know what time it is
in fact i just checked
i even know the date
and the month and the year
i know i haven't been sleeping
and when i do
i just dream of you dear

i miss watching you drool on your pillow
i miss watching you pull on your clothes
i miss listening to you in the bathroom
flushing the toilet blowing your nose

i'm calling from the diner
the diner on the corner
i ordered two coffees
one is for you
and the cups are so close
that the steam is rising
in one stream
how are you

i think yer the least fucked up
person i've ever met
and that may be as close to the real thing
as i'm ever gonna get
but my quarter's gonna run out now
or so i'm told i
guess i'd better go sit down
i will wait for you
'til my coffee gets cold

# THE DINER

**Words and Music by Ani DiFranco**

the di - ner on the cor - ner. ___ I or-dered two cof - fees. ___ One is for you. __

C#m7b5b9             C#m7 Cm7 Bm7    A$_6^7$                            Em7add9

And the cups are so close     that the steam is ris - ing in one       stream. ___

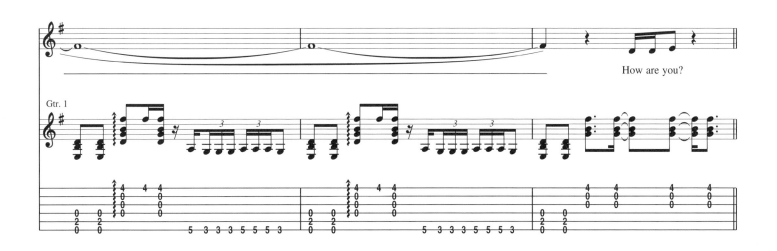

How are you?

Gtr. 1

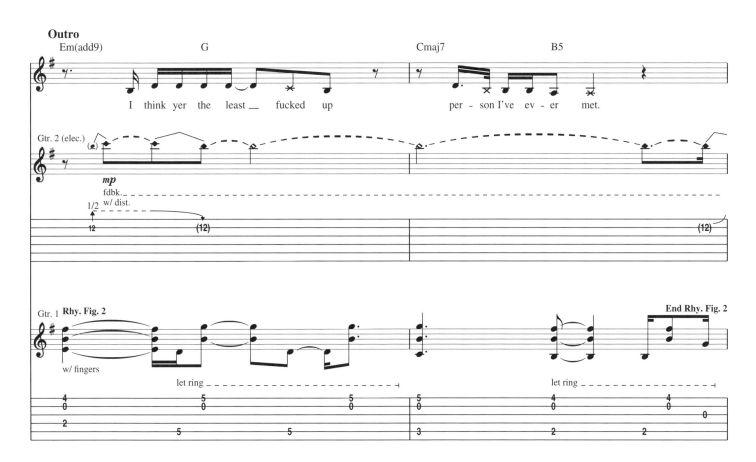

**Outro**

Em(add9)             G                              Cmaj7             B5

I think yer the least ___ fucked up       per - son I've ev - er met.

Gtr. 2 (elec.)

*mp*

fdbk.

w/ dist.

1/2

Gtr. 1  **Rhy. Fig. 2**                                                            **End Rhy. Fig. 2**

w/ fingers

let ring ___                                         let ring ___

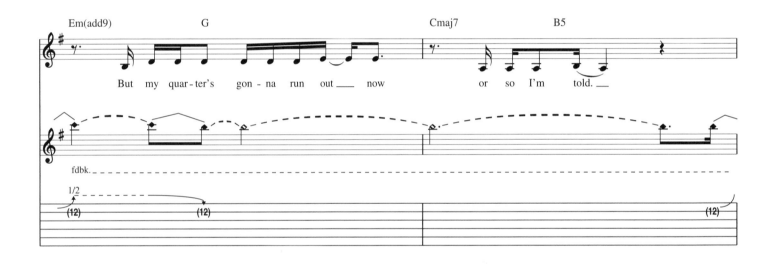

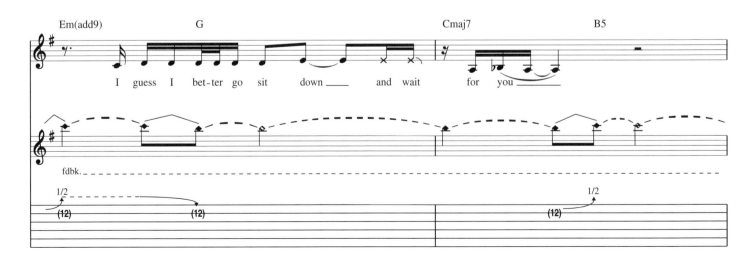

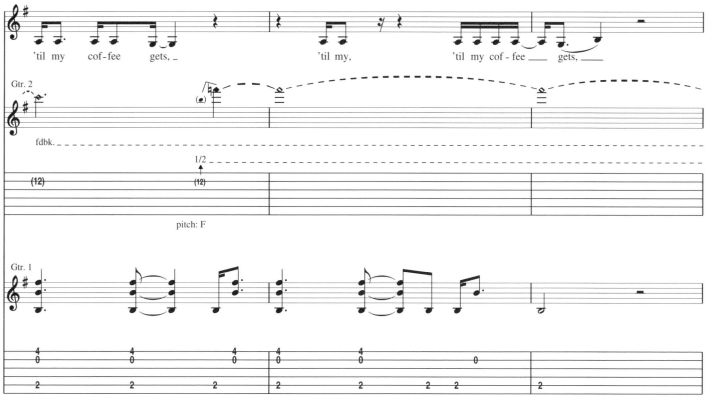

'til my cof-fee gets, \_ 'til my, 'til my cof-fee \_ gets, \_

Gtr. 2

fdbk. ----------------------------------------

1/2

(12) (12)

pitch: F

Gtr. 1

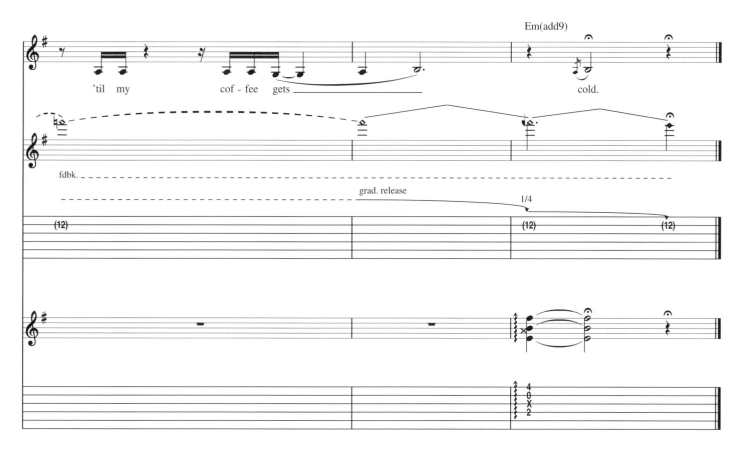

Em(add9)

'til my cof-fee gets _____ cold.

fdbk. -----------------------

grad. release

1/4

(12) (12) (12)

she's looking in the mirror
she's fixing her hair
and i touch my head
to feel what isn't there
she's humming a melody
we learned in grade school
she's so happy and i think
this is not cool
'cause i know the guy
she's been talking about
i have met him before
and i think what is this
beautiful woman settling for
she bends her breath
when she talks to him
i can see her features begin to blur
as she pours herself
into the mold he made for her
and for everything he does
she has a way to rationalize
she tells me he don't mean
what he do
she tells me he called
to apologize
he says he loves her
he says he's changing
and he can keep her warm
she sits there like america
suffering through slow reform
but she'll never get back the time
and the years sneak by
one by one
she is still playing the martyr
and i am still praying
for a revolution
she still doesn't have what she deserves
but she wakes up smiling everyday
she never really expected more
that's just not the way
we are raised
and i say to her
you know, there's plenty
of really great men out there
but she doesn't hear me
she's looking in the mirror
she's fixing her hair

FIXING HER HAIR

from *Imperfectly*

# FIXING HER HAIR

### Words and Music by Ani DiFranco

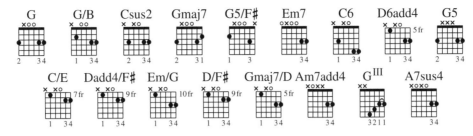

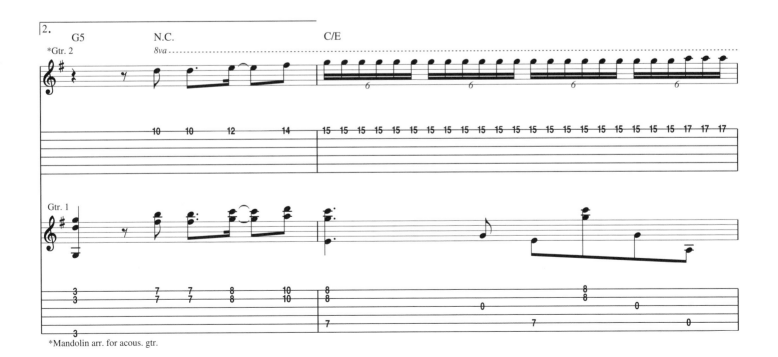

*Mandolin arr. for acous. gtr.

**33**

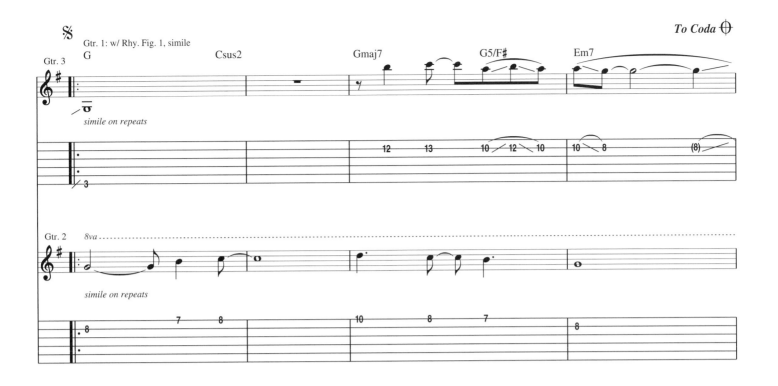

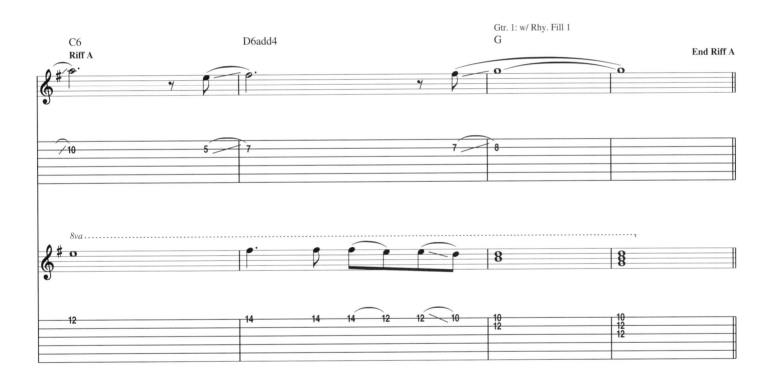

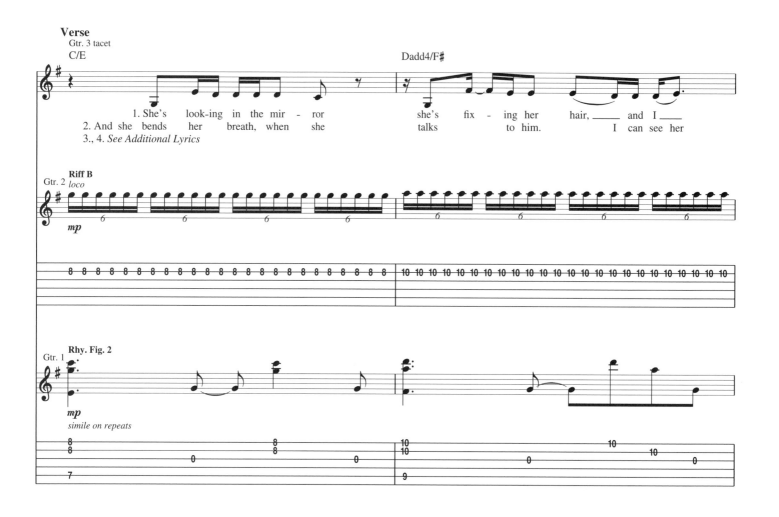

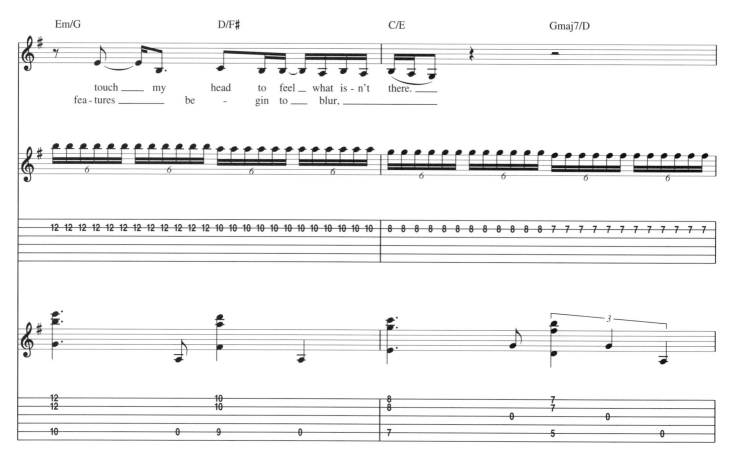

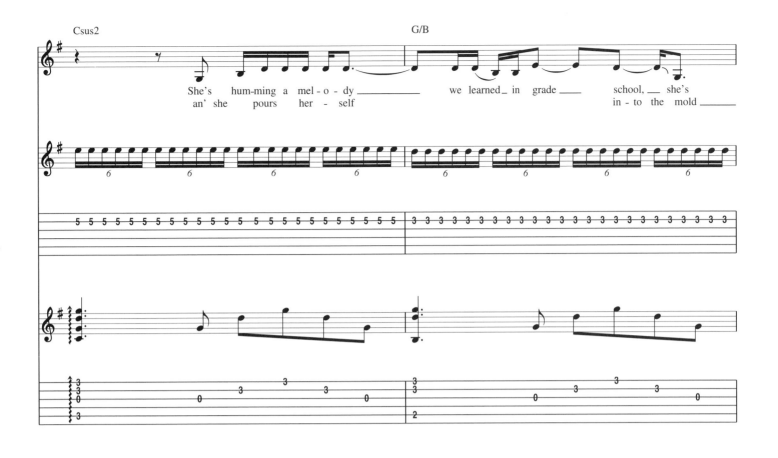

She's hum-ming a mel-o-dy ___ we learned in grade ___ school, ___ she's
an' she pours her-self in-to the mold ___

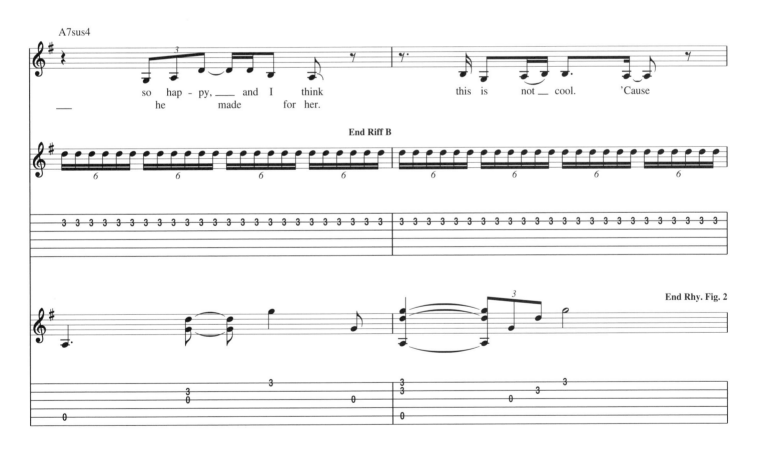

so hap-py, ___ and I think this is not ___ cool. 'Cause
he made for her.

End Riff B

End Rhy. Fig. 2

Gtr. 1: w/ Rhy. Fig. 2, simile
Gtr. 2: w/ Riff A, simile

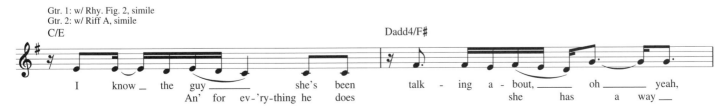

I know ___ the guy ___ she's been talk - ing a - bout, oh ___ yeah,
An' for ev-'ry-thing he does she has a way ___

I have met him be-fore. _____
to ra-tion-al-ize. _____

And I think what is _____ this
She tells me he don't

4th time, D.S. al Coda

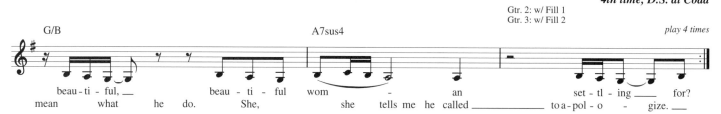

Gtr. 2: w/ Fill 1
Gtr. 3: w/ Fill 2

*play 4 times*

beau-ti-ful, _____    beau-ti-ful wom - an    set-tl-ing _____ for?
mean what he do.    She,    she tells me he called _____ to a-pol-o - gize. _____

### ⊕ *Coda*

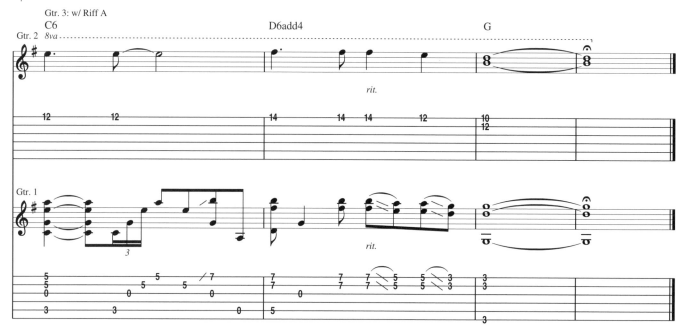

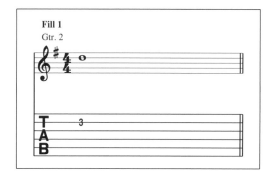

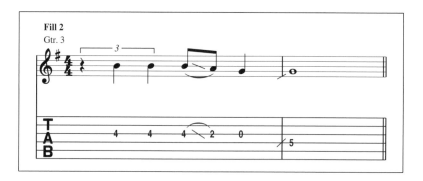

*Additional Lyrics*

3. And he says he loves her, he says he's changing,
   And he can keep her warm.
   And she sits there like America,
   Suffering through slow reform.
   But she'll never get back the time,
   And the years sneak by one by one.
   She is still playing the martyr,
   And I am still praying for a revolution.

4. And she still doesn't have what she deserves,
   But she wakes up smiling every day.
   She never really expected more,
   That's just not the way we are raised.
   And I say to her, "You know,
   There's plenty of really great men out there."
   But she doesn't hear me, she's looking in the mirror;
   She's fixing her hair.

# GOD'S COUNTRY

state trooper  thinks i drive
too fast
pulled me over to tell me so
i say out here on the prairie
any speed is too slow
i miss brooklyn i miss my crew
let's start over i missed my cue
guess i forgot
who i was talking to
i should have recognized
that fierce look in his eyes
i've seen it in my mirror
so many times
he's gonna put two
cents in

'cause he's got a gun
but i'm gonna put in three
'cause history owes me one
guess i came out here
to see some stuff
for myself
i mean why leave the telling
up to everybody else
this may be god's country
but this is my country too
move over mr. holiness
let the little people thru
thank you
for serving and protecting
the likes of me

thanks for the ticket
now can i leave
you know i have left
everywhere that i have
ever been
i don't really recommend
it though
not like anybody asked me
maybe you and i
will meet again  some day
i've been known to
come down this road
maybe it's destiny
and then again
maybe not, i don't know

# GOD'S COUNTRY

### Words and Music by Ani DiFranco

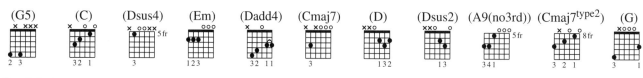

(G5)  (C)  (Dsus4)  (Em)  (Dadd4)  (Cmaj7)  (D)  (Dsus2)  (A9(no3rd))  (Cmaj7^type2)  (G)

Drop D Tuning, Capo IV:
① = E   ④ = D
② = B   ⑤ = A
③ = G   ⑥ = D

**Intro**
**Moderately** ♩ = 132

*Symbols in parentheses represent chord names respective to capoed guitar.
Symbols above reflect actual sounding chords. Capoed fret is "0" in tab.

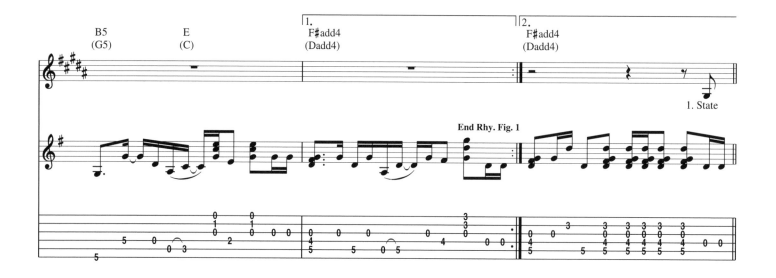

𝄋 **Verse**

Gtr. 1: w/ Rhy. Fig. 1, 2 times, 1st time, simile
Gtr. 1: w/ Rhy. Fig. 1, 1st 2 meas., 3 times, 2nd, 3rd & 4th times, simile

troop - er  thinks __ I  drive  too  fast,  pulled me  o - ver  to  tell  me  so. __
rec - og - nized __ that __ fierce  look  in  his __ eyes;  I've

3., 5. *See Additional Lyrics*

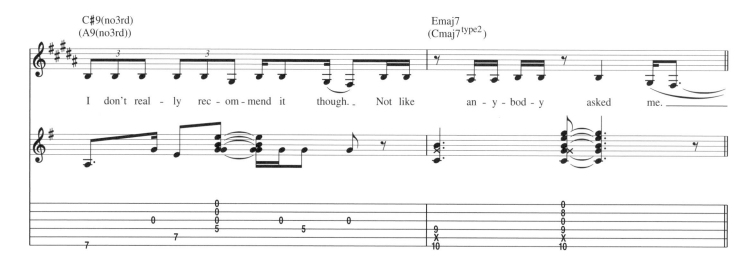

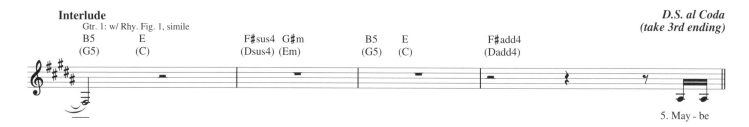

**Interlude**
Gtr. 1: w/ Rhy. Fig. 1, simile

*D.S. al Coda
(take 3rd ending)*

| B5 | E | | F#sus4 G#m | | B5 | E | | F#add4 | |
|----|----|----|----|----|----|----|----|----|----|
| (G5) | (C) | | (Dsus4) (Em) | | (G5) | (C) | | (Dadd4) | |

5. May - be

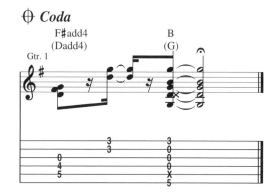

⊕ *Coda*

F#add4    B
(Dadd4)    (G)
Gtr. 1

*Additional Lyrics*

3. Guess I came out here to see some stuff for myself.
I mean, why leave the telling up to everybody else?
This may be God's country but this is my country too.
Move over, Mr. Holiness, let the little people through.

5. Maybe you and I will meet again someday.
I've been known to come down this road.
Maybe it is destiny and then again, maybe not.
I don't know.

# IF HE TRIES ANYTHING

i'm invincible
so are you
we do all the things
they say we can't do
we walk around
in the middle of the night
and if it's too far to walk
we just hitch a ride

we got rings of dirt
around our necks
we talk like auctioneers
and we bounce like checks
we smell like shit
still when we walk down the street
all the boys line up
to throw themselves at our feet

i say i think he likes you
you say i think he do too
i say go and get him girl
before he gets you
i'll be watching from the wings
i will come to your rescue
if he tries anything

it's a long long road
it's a big big world
we are wise wise women
we are giggling girls
we both carry a smile
to show when we're pleased
we both carry a switchblade
in our sleeves

tell you one thing
i'm going to make noise when i go down
for ten square blocks
they're gonna know i died
all the goddesses will come up
to the ripped screen door
and say what do you want dear
and i'll say i want inside

i say i think he likes you
you say i think he do too
i say go and get him girl
before he gets you
i'll be watching you from the wings
i will come to your rescue
if he tries anything

from *Out of Range*

# IF HE TRIES ANYTHING

**Words and Music by Ani DiFranco**

*Slap strings with right hand.

## Additional Lyrics

3. It's a long, long road,
   It's a big, big world.
   We are wise, wise women,
   We are giggling girls.
   We both carry a smile
   To show when we're pleased.
   We both carry a switchblade
   In our sleeves.

4. Tell you one thing
   I'm going to make noise when I go down
   For ten square blocks
   They're gonna know I died.
   All the goddesses will come up
   To the ripped screen door
   And say, "What do you want dear?"
   And I'll say, "I want inside."

iN oR OuT

guess there's something wrong with me
guess i don't fit in
no one wants to touch it
no one knows where to begin
i've got more than one membership
to more than one club
and i owe my life
to the people that i love

he looks me up and down
like he knows what time it is
like he's got my number
like he thinks it's his
he says call me miss difranco
if there's anything i can do
i say it's mr. difranco to you

some days the line i walk
turns out to be straight
other days the line tends to deviate
i've got no criteria for sex or race
i just want to hear your voice
i just want to see your face

she looks me up and down
like she thinks that i'll mature
like she's got my number
like it belongs to her
she says call me ms. difranco
if there's anything i can do
i say i've got spots
i've got stripes too

their eyes are all asking
are you in or are you out
and i think, oh man
what is this about
tonight you can't put me
up on any shelf
because i came here alone
and i'm going to leave by myself

i just want to show you
the way that i feel
and when i get tired
you can take the wheel
to me what's more important
is the person that i bring
not just getting to the same restaurant
and eating the same thing

# IN OR OUT

### Words and Music by Ani DiFranco

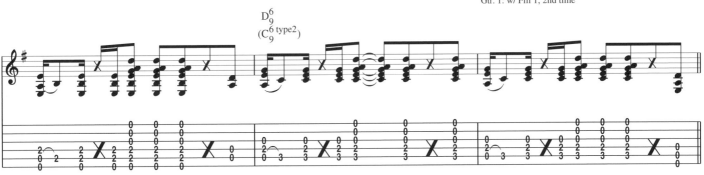

## Verse

1. Guess there's some-thing wrong with me, ___ guess I don't fit in.
2. Some days the line I walk turns out to be straight.

2., 4. *See Additional Lyrics*

No one wants_ to touch it, ___ no one ___ knows where _ to be - gin. ___ I've ___ got
Oth - er days the line tends to de - vi - ate. I've ___ got

more than ___ one mem - ber - ship to more than ___ one club. _____ And I,
no cri - te - ri - a for sex or race. I just want to

I owe ___ my life ___ to the peo - ple that ___ I love. ___ He
hear your voice, I just want to see your face.

looks me up ___ and down ___ like he knows what time it is, like he's
She looks me up and down ___ like she thinks that I'll ma - ture, like she's

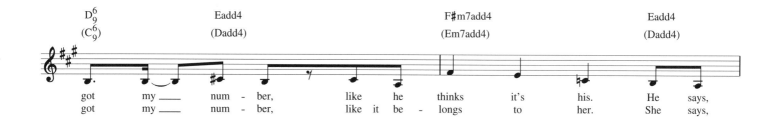

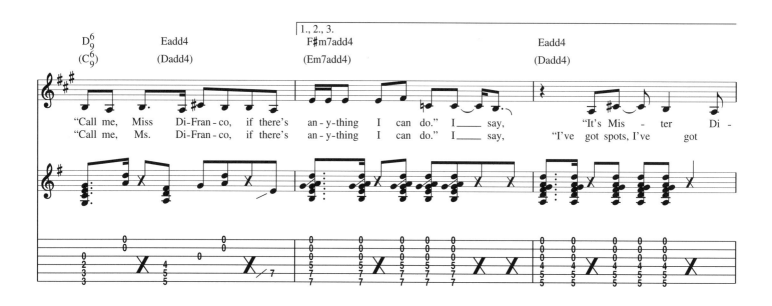

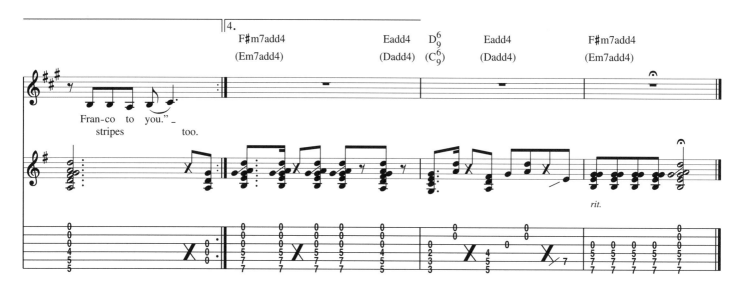

*Additional Lyrics*

3. Their eyes are all asking, "Are you in or are you out?"
And I think, oh man, what is this about?
I mean, tonight you can't put me up on any shelf,
'Cause I came here alone, and I'm gonna leave by myself.
I just want to show you the way that I feel,
And when I get tired, you can take the wheel.
To me what's more important is the person that I bring,
Not just getting to the same restaurant and eating the same thing.

4. Guess there's something wrong with me, guess I don't fit in.
No one wants to touch it, no one knows where to begin.
I've got more than one membership to more than one club.
And I, I owe my life to the people that I love.

# JOYFUL GIRL

i do it for the joy it brings
because i'm a joyful girl
because the world owes me nothing
and we owe each other the world
i do it because it's the least i can do
i do it because i learned it from you
and i do it just because i want to
because i want to

everything i do is judged
and they mostly get it wrong
but oh well
'cuz the bathroom mirror has not budged
and the woman who lives there can tell
the truth from the stuff that they say
and she looks me in the eye
and says would you prefer the easy way
no, well o.k. then
don't cry

i wonder if everything i do
i do instead
of something i want to do more
the question fills my head
i know there's no grand plan here
this is just the way it goes
when everything else seems unclear
i guess at least i know

i do it for the joy it brings
because i'm a joyful girl
because the world owes me nothing
and we owe each other the world
i do it because it's the least i can do
i do it because i learned it from you
and i do it just because i want to
because i want to

from *Dilate*

# JOYFUL GIRL

### Words and Music by Ani DiFranco

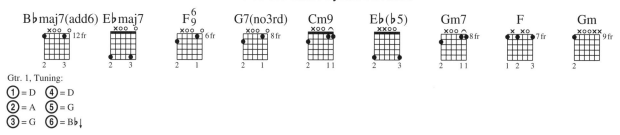

Gtr. 1, Tuning:
① = D   ④ = D
② = A   ⑤ = G
③ = G   ⑥ = B♭↓

**Intro**
Slowly ♩. = 52

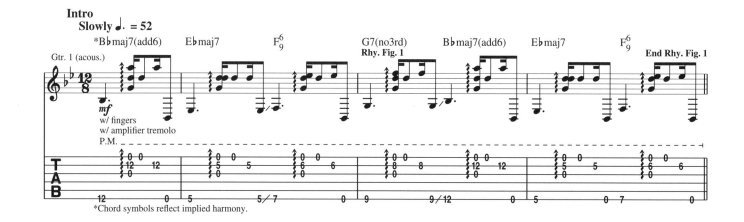

*Chord symbols reflect implied harmony.

**Verse**

Gtr. 1: w/ Rhy. Fig. 1, 5 times, 1st time, simile
Gtr. 1: w/ Rhy. Fig. 1, 4 times, 2nd time, simile

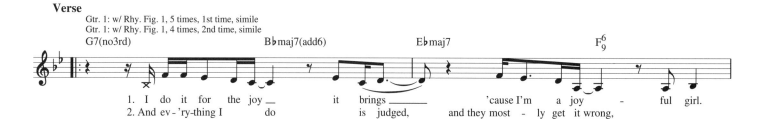

1. I do it for the joy ___ it brings ___ 'cause I'm a joy - ful girl.
2. And ev - 'ry-thing I do is judged, and they most - ly get it wrong,

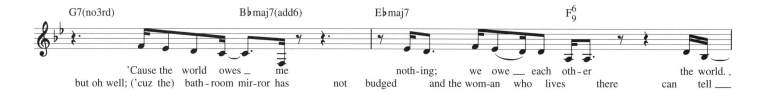

'Cause the world owes ___ me noth-ing; we owe ___ each oth-er the world.
but oh well; ('cuz the) bath-room mir-ror has not budged and the wom-an who lives there can tell ___

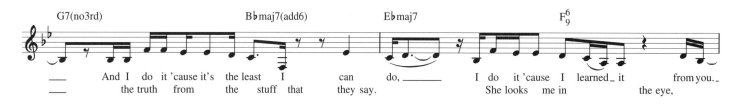

___ And I do it 'cause it's the least I can do, ___ I do it 'cause I learned ___ it from you.
___ the truth from the stuff that they say. She looks me in the eye,

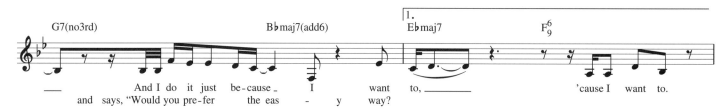

___ And I do it just be-cause ___ I want to, ___ 'cause I want to.
and says, "Would you pre - fer the eas - y way?"

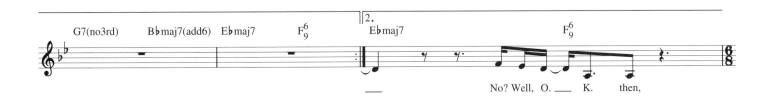

No? Well, O. K. then,

**Interlude**

don't cry.    Na, ah. _____    Hey, ah, _____    hey, _____

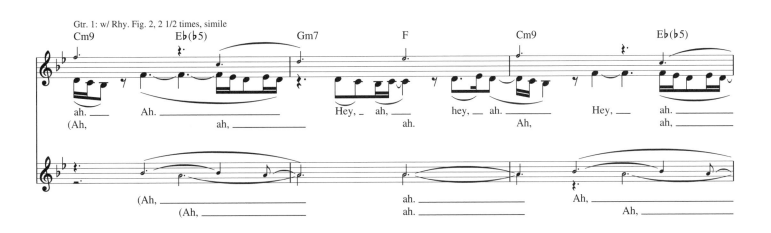

ah.    Ah. _____    ah, _____    Hey, ah,    ah.    hey, ah.    Hey, _____    ah.    
(Ah,    ah,    ah.    Ah,    ah,

(Ah, _____    (Ah, _____    ah. _____    Ah, _____    Ah,
                                            (Ah, _____    ah. _____    Ah, _____

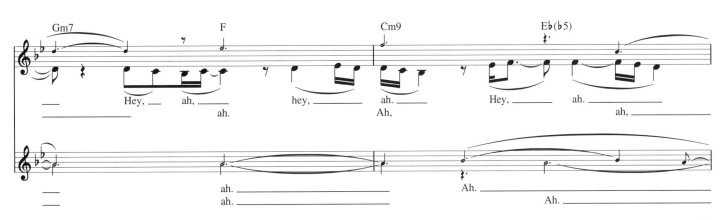

_____    Hey, _____ ah,    hey, _____    ah.    Hey, _____    ah.
                ah.    Ah,    ah, _____

_____    ah. _____    Ah. _____    Ah. _____
                ah. _____    Ah. _____

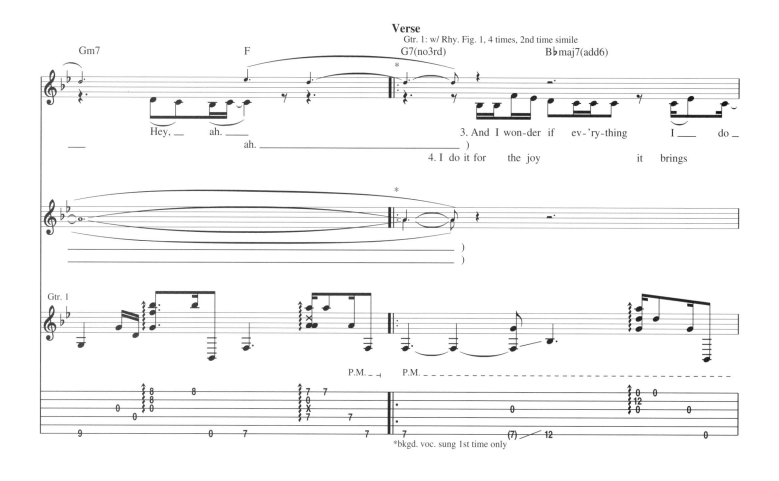

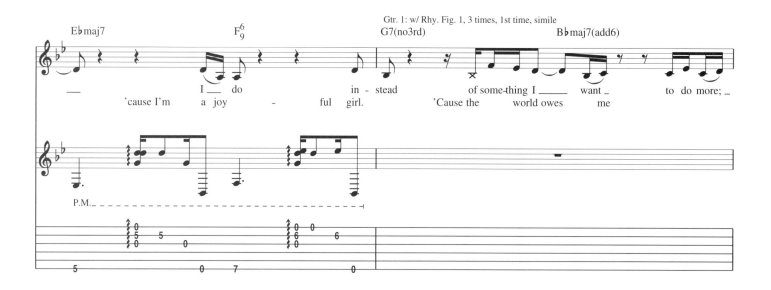

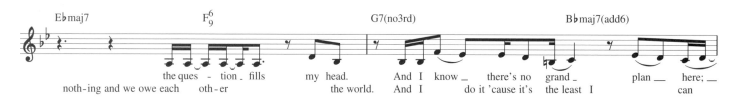

this is just the way__ it__ goes.__ And when ev-'ry-thing else__ seems

do and I do it 'cause I learned it from you. I do it just be-cause I

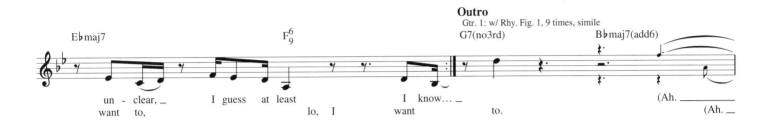

**Outro**
Gtr. 1: w/ Rhy. Fig. 1, 9 times, simile

un - clear,__ I guess at least I know...__ (Ah.__

want to, lo, I want to. (Ah.__

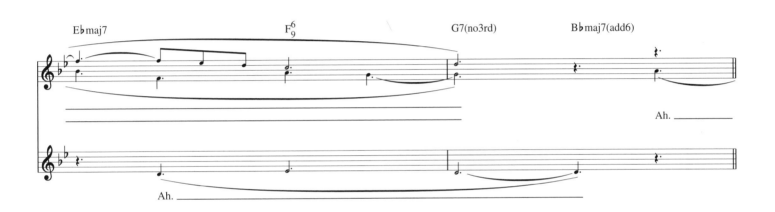

Ah.__

Ah.__

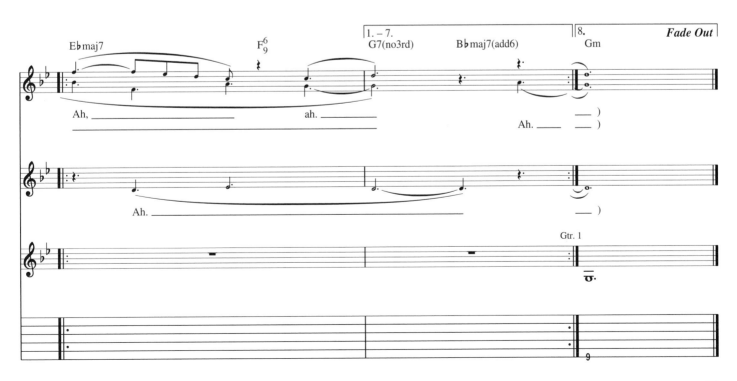

Ah,__ ah.__

Ah.__

Gtr. 1

don't ask me why i'm crying
i'm not gonna tell you what's wrong
i'm just gonna sit on your lap
for five dollars a song
i want you to pay me for my beauty
i think it's only right
'cause i have been paying for it
all of my life

i'm gonna take the money i make
and i'm gonna go away

we barely have time to react in this world
let alone rehearse
and i don't think that i'm better than you
but i don't think that i'm worse
women learn to be women
and men learn to be men
and i don't blame it all on you
but i don't want to be your friend

i'm gonna take the money i make
and i'm gonna go away

i was eleven years old
he was as old as my dad
and he took something from me
i didn't even know that i had
so don't tell me about decency
don't tell me about pride
just give me something for my trouble
'cause this time it's not a free ride

i'm just gonna take the money i make
and i'm gonna go away

don't ask me why i'm crying
i'm not gonna tell you what's wrong
i'm just gonna sit on your lap
for five dollars a song
i want you to pay me for my beauty
i think it's only right
'cause i have been paying for it
all of my life
now i just wanna take
i'm just gonna take
i'm gonna take
and i'm gonna go away

LETTER TO A JOHN

# LETTER TO A JOHN

**Words and Music by Ani DiFranco**

*Symbols in parentheses represent chord names respective to capoed guitar. Symbols above reflect
actual sounding chords. Capoed fret is "0" in tab. Chord symbols reflect overall harmony.

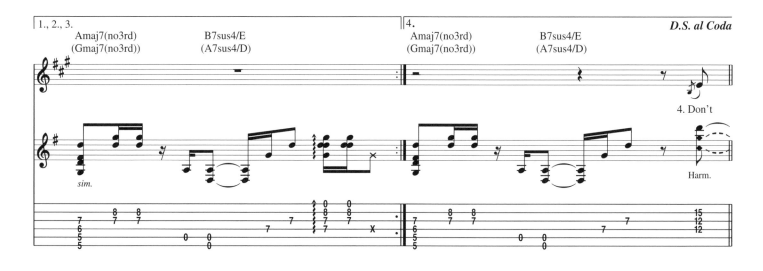

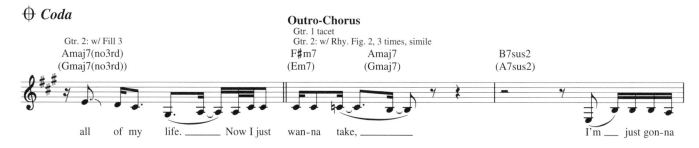

## ⊕ *Coda*

**Outro-Chorus**

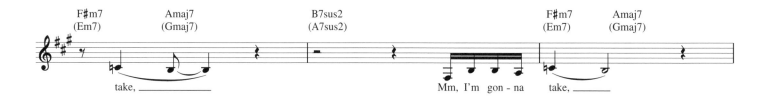

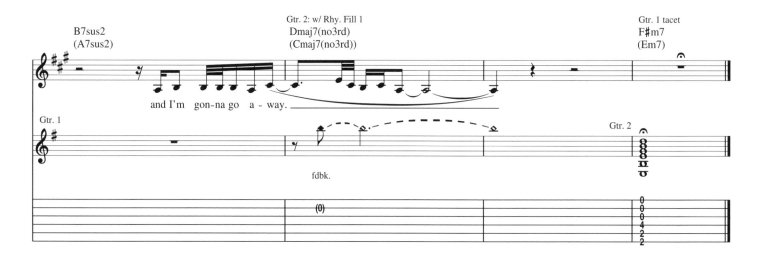

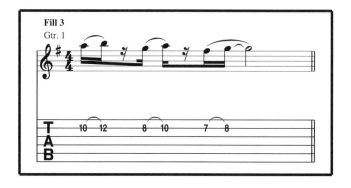

NOₜ A PₚₑₜₜY GₒRL

i am not a pretty girl
that is not what i do
i ain't no damsel in distress
and i don't need to be rescued
so put me down punk
wouldn't you prefer a maiden fair
isn't there a kitten
stuck up a tree somewhere

i am not an angry girl
but it seems like
i've got everyone fooled
every time i say something
they find hard to hear
they chalk it up to my anger
never to their own fear

imagine you're a girl
just trying to finally come clean
knowing full well they'd prefer
you were dirty
and smiling
i'm sorry
but i am not a maiden fair
and i am not a kitten
stuck up a tree somewhere

generally my generation
wouldn't be caught dead
working for the man
and generally i agree with them
trouble is you got to have yourself
an alternate plan
i have earned my disillusionment
i have been working all of my life
i am a patriot
i have been fighting the good fight
and what if there are
no damsels in distress

what if i knew that
and i called your bluff
don't you think every kitten
figures out how to get down
whether or not you ever show up

i am not a pretty girl
i don't really want to be a pretty girl
i want to be more than a pretty girl

from *Not a Pretty Girl*

# NOT A PRETTY GIRL

**Words and Music by Ani DiFranco**

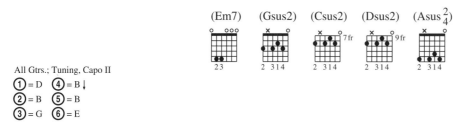

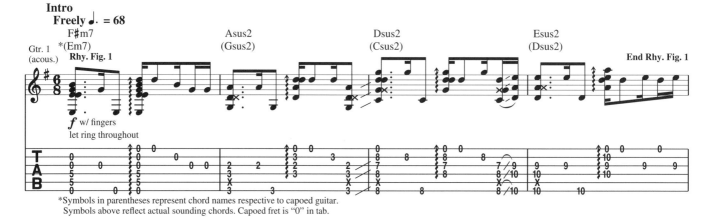

*Symbols in parentheses represent chord names respective to capoed guitar.
Symbols above reflect actual sounding chords. Capoed fret is "0" in tab.

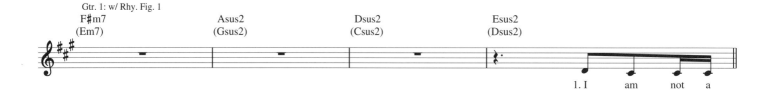

1. I am not a

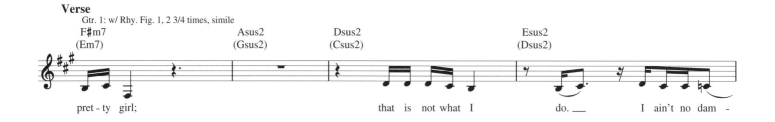

pret-ty girl;     that is not what I     do. ___     I ain't no dam-

-sel in dis-tress     and I don't need     to be ___ res-cued,

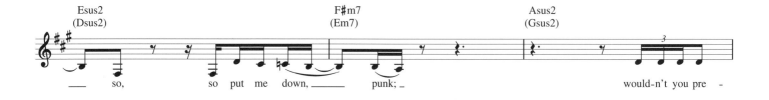

___ so,     so put me down, ___ punk; _     would-n't you pre-

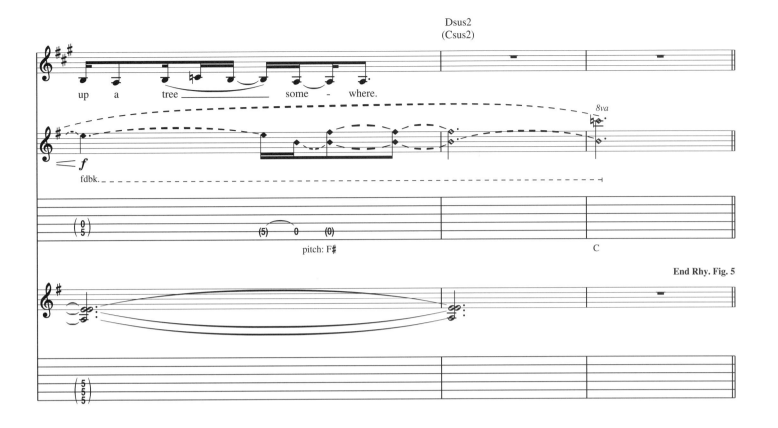

**Interlude**

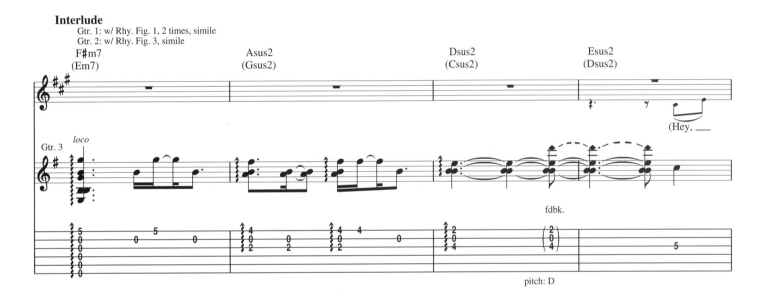

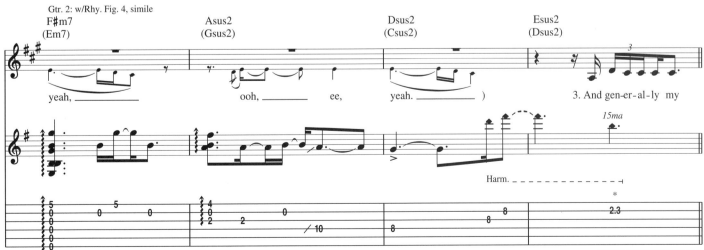

*Harmonic located between
2nd & 3rd frets.

**Chorus**

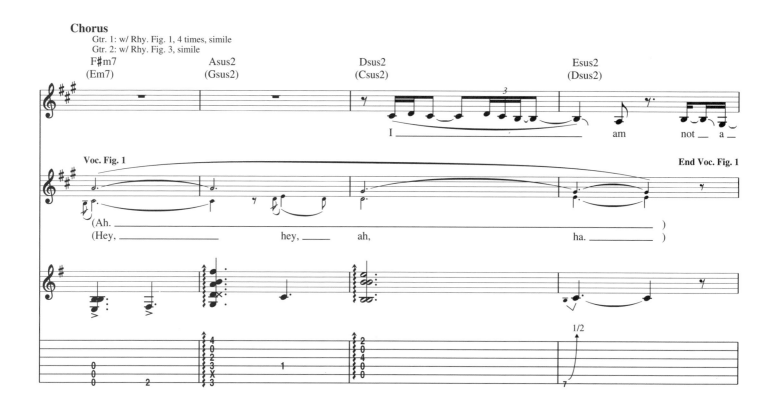

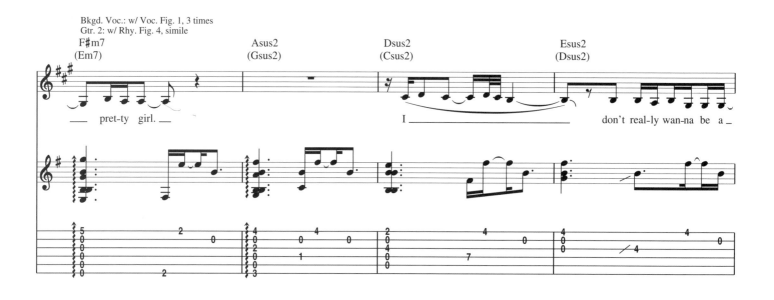

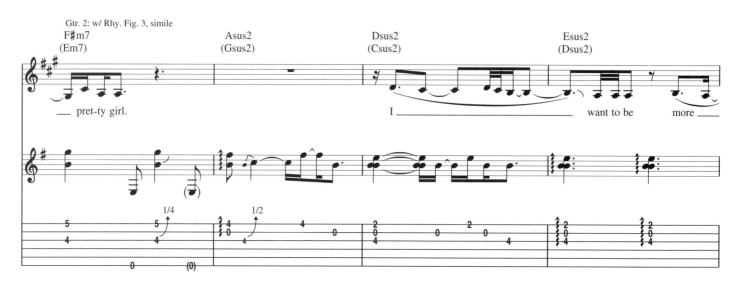

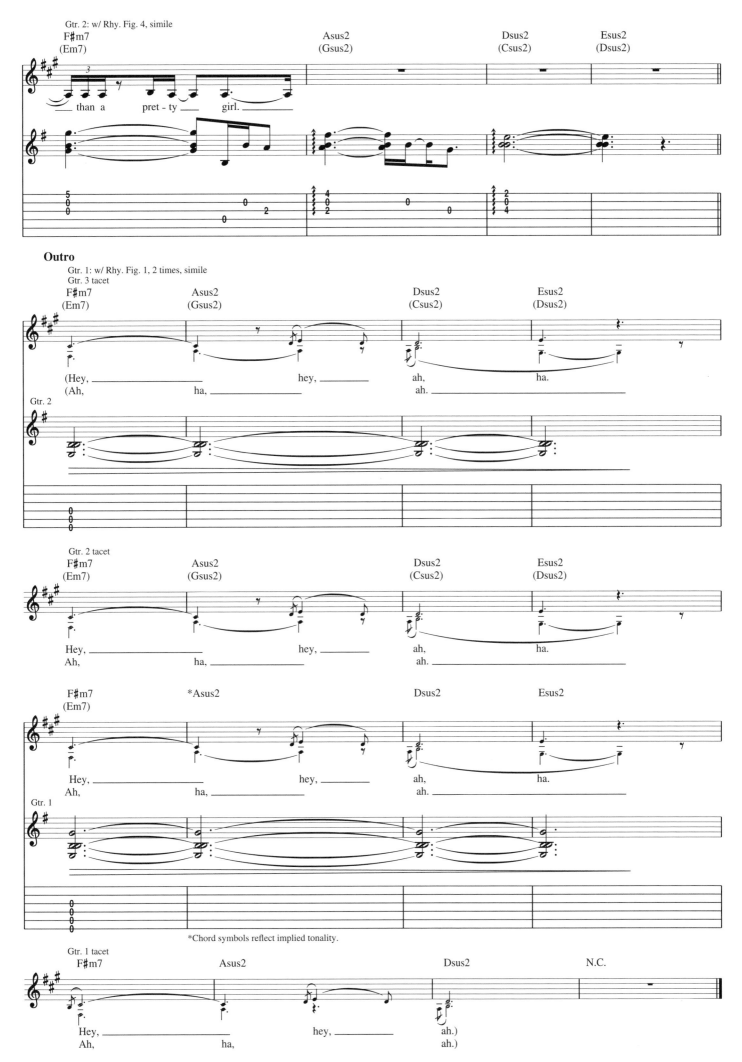

**Outro**

*Chord symbols reflect implied tonality.

# OUT OF HABIT

the butter melts out of habit
the toast isn't even warm
the waitress and the man in the plaid shirt
play out a scene they've played
so many times before
i am watching the sun
stumble home in the morning
from a bar on the east side of town
and the coffee is just water dressed in brown
beautiful but boring he visited me yesterday
he noticed my fingers
and he asked me if i would play
i didn't really care a lot
but i couldn't think of a reason why not
i said if you don't come any closer
i don't mind if you stay
my thighs have been involved
in many accidents
and now i can't get insured
and i don't need to be lured by you

my cunt is built
like a wound that won't heal
now you don't have to ask
because you know how i feel
art is why i get up in the morning
but my definition ends there
it doesn't seem fair
that i'm living for something
i can't even define
there you are right there
in the meantime
i don't want to play for you anymore
show me what you can do
tell me what are you here for
i want my old friends
i want my old face
i want my old mind
fuck this time and place
the butter melts out of habit
the toast isn't even warm

from *Ani DiFranco*

# OUT OF HABIT

**Words and Music by Ani DiFranco**

you an-y more. ____ Show me what you can __ do, __ tell me what are you __ here __ for.

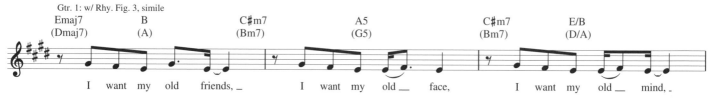

Gtr. 1: w/ Rhy. Fig. 3, simile

I want my old friends, _ I want my old __ face, I want my old __ mind, _

**Chorus**

Gtr. 1: w/ Rhy. Fig. 3, simile

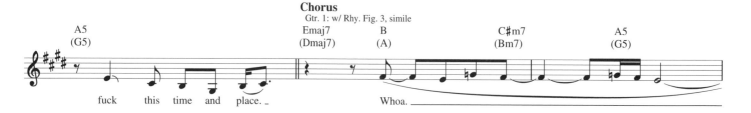

fuck this time and place. _ Whoa. _____

Gtr. 1: w/ Rhy. Fig. 2

__ Whoa, _____

**Outro**

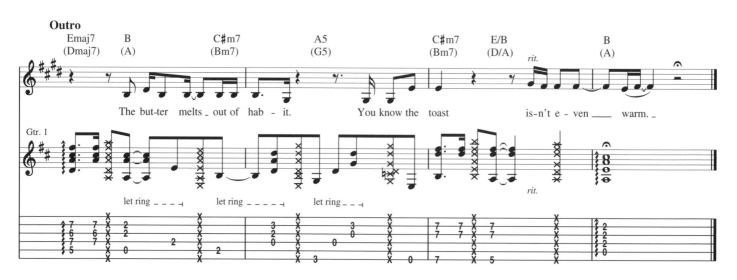

The but-ter melts _ out of hab - it. You know the toast is-n't e - ven __ warm. _

let ring _ _ _ _    let ring _ _ _ _    let ring _ _ _

Gtr. 1

# OUT OF RANGE

i was locked
into being my mother's daughter
i was just eating bread and water
thinking nothing ever changes
then i was shocked
to see the mistakes of each generation
will just fade like a radio station
if you drive out of range

just the thought of our bed
makes me crumble like the plaster
where you punched the wall
beside my head
and i try to draw the line
but it ends up running
down the middle of me
most of the time

baby i love you
that's why i'm leaving
there's just no talking to you
and there's just no pleasing you
and i care enough
that i'm mad
that half the world don't even know
what they could'a had

just the thought of our bed
makes me crumble like the plaster
where you punched the wall
beside my head
and i try to draw the line
but it ends up running
down the middle of me
most of the time
boys get locked up
in some prison
girls get locked up
in some house
and it don't matter
if it's a warden
or a lover or a spouse
you just can't talk to 'em
you just can't reason
you just can't leave
and you just can't please 'em
i was locked
into being my mother's daughter
i was just eating bread and water
thinking nothing ever changes
then i was shocked
to see the mistakes of each generation
will just fade like a radio station
if you drive out of range

i was locked
into being my mother's daughter
i was just eating bread and water
thinking nothing ever changes
then i was shocked
to see the mistakes of each generation
will just fade like a radio station
if you drive
you just gotta drive
out of range

if you're not angry
then you're just stupid
or you don't care
how else can you react
when you know
something's so unfair
when the men of the hour
can kill half the world in war
or make them
slaves to a superpower
and then let them die poor

from *Out of Range*

# OUT OF RANGE (ACOUSTIC)

**Words and Music by Ani DiFranco**

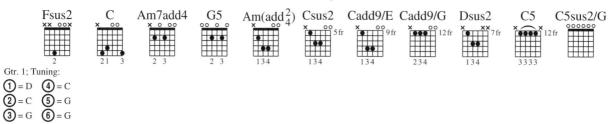

Gtr. 1; Tuning:
① = D  ④ = C
② = C  ⑤ = G
③ = G  ⑥ = G

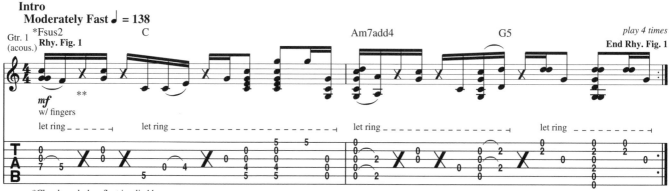

*Chord symbols reflect implied harmony.
**Tap face of guitar with right hand.

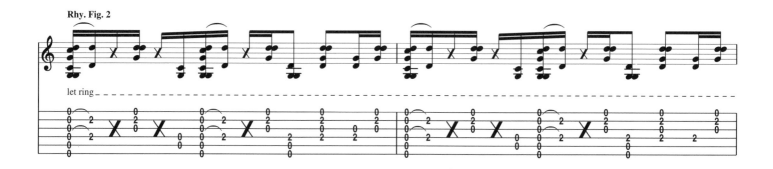

*Slap strings with right hand.

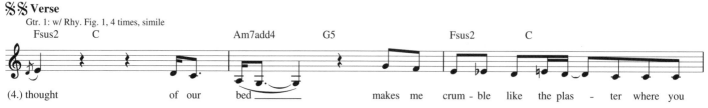

(4.) thought          of our          bed _____ makes me  crum-ble  like  the  plas - ter  where you

78

punched the wall _ be - side _ my head. _ And I try to draw the line, _ but it ends up

Gtr. 1: w/ Rhy. Fig. 2, last 2 meas., simile

run-ning down _ the mid-dle of ___ me most of the time. _____

2. And boys get
5. And ba-by I

## 𝄉 Verse
Gtr. 1: w/ Rhy. Fig. 1, 4 times, simile

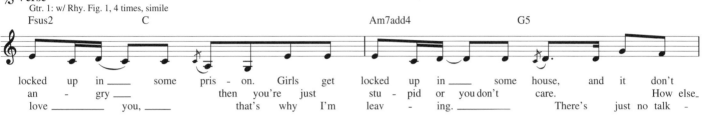

locked up in ___ some pris - on. Girls get locked up in ___ some house, and it don't
an - gry ___ then you're just stu - pid or you don't care. How else _
love ___ you, ___ that's why I'm leav - ing. _____ There's just no talk -

mat - ter if it's ___ a war - den, ___ or a lov - er, or a spouse. _____ You just
___ can you ___ re - act ___ when you know some - thing's so un - fair? When the
- ing to you ___ and there's just no pleas - ing you. And I care e - nough _

can't talk ___ to 'em. You just ___ can't rea - son. You just ___ can't _____
men of the hour ___ can kill half the world in war or make them
___ that I'm mad that half the world _____

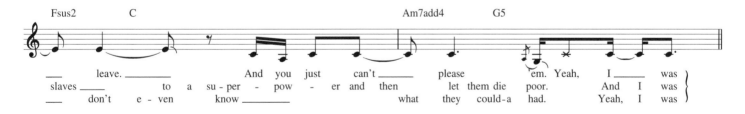

___ leave. _____ And you just can't please 'em. Yeah, I was
slaves ___ to a su - per - pow - er and then let them die poor. And I was
___ don't e - ven know _____ what they could-a had. Yeah, I was

## Chorus

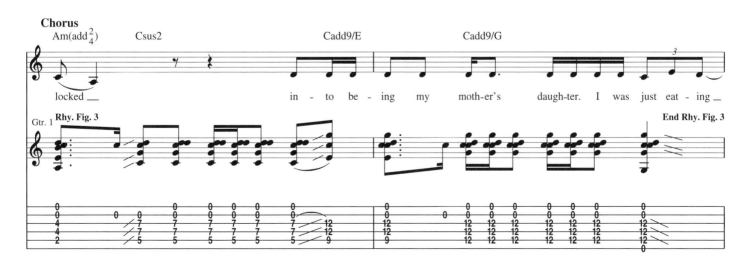

locked ___ in - to be - ing my moth-er's daugh-ter. I was just eat-ing _

Gtr. 1  **Rhy. Fig. 3**

**End Rhy. Fig. 3**

Gtr. 1: w/ Rhy. Fig. 3, 2 times, simile

\_ bread and \_ wa - ter think - ing noth - ing ev - er chan - ges. And I was \_

\_ shocked to see the mis - takes of each gen - er - a - tion will just fade \_

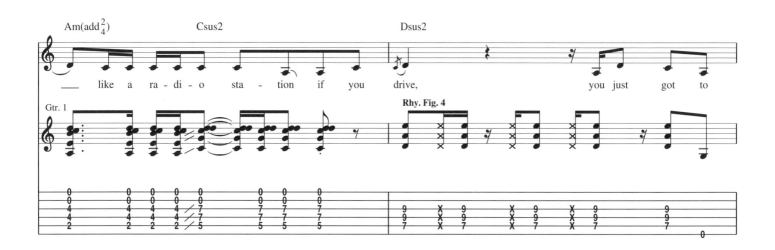

\_ like a ra - di - o sta - tion if you drive, you just got to

Gtr. 1

**Rhy. Fig. 4**

*To Coda* ⊕

Gtr. 1: w/ Rhy. Fill 1, 2nd time

C5

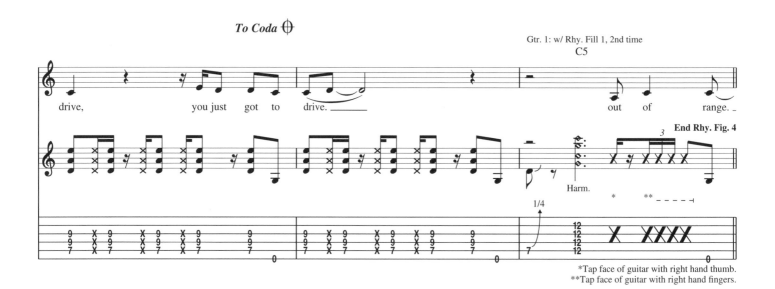

drive, you just got to drive. \_ out of range. \_

**End Rhy. Fig. 4**

Harm.

1/4

*Tap face of guitar with right hand thumb.
**Tap face of guitar with right hand fingers.

**Rhy. Fill 1**

Gtr. 1

Harm.

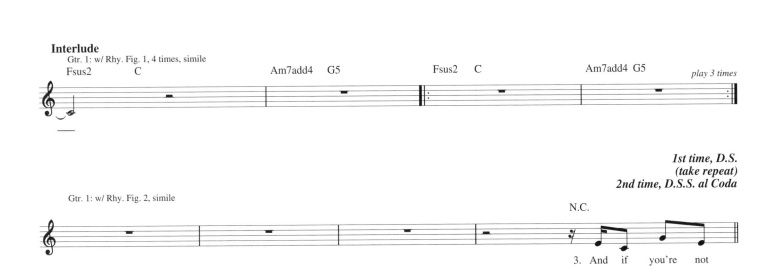

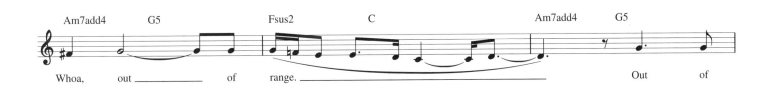

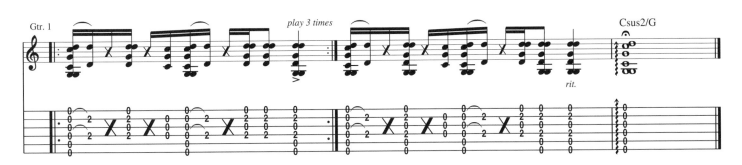

SHAMELES

i cannot name this
i cannot explain this
and i really don't want to
just call me shameless
i can't even slow this down
let alone stop this
and i keep looking around
but i cannot top this

if i had any sense
i guess i'd fear this
i guess i'd keep it down
so no one would hear this
i guess i'd shut my mouth
and rethink a minute
but i can't shut it now
'cuz there's something in it

we're in a room without a door
and i am sure without a doubt
they're gonna wanna know
how we got in here
and they're gonna wanna know
how we plan to get out
we better have a good explanation
for all the fun that we had
'cuz they are coming for us, babe
and they are going to be mad
yeah they're going to be mad at us

this is my skeleton
this is the skin it's in
that is, according to light
and gravity
i'll take off my disguise
the mask you met me in

'cuz i got something
for you to see
just gimme your skeleton
give me the skin it's in
yeah baby, this is you
according to me
i never avert my eyes
i never compromise
so never mind
the poetry

i gotta cover my butt 'cuz i covet
another man's wife
i gotta divide my emotions
into wrong and right
then i get to see how close i can get to it
without giving in
then i get to rub up against it
'til i break the skin
rub up against it
'til i break the skin

they're gonna be mad at us
they're gonna be mad at me and you
they're gonna be mad at us
and all the things
we wanna do

just please don't name this
please don't explain this
just blame it all on me
say i was shameless
say i couldn't slow it down
let alone stop it
and say you just hung around
'cuz you couldn't top it

from *Dilate*

# SHAMELESS

**Words and Music by Ani DiFranco**

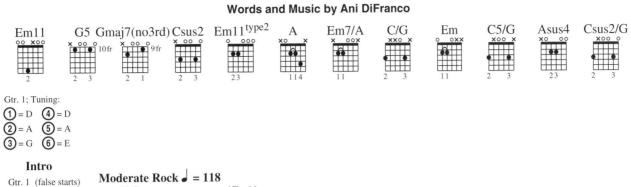

Gtr. 1; Tuning:
①= D  ④= D
②= A  ⑤= A
③= G  ⑥= E

**Intro**

Gtr. 1 (false starts)
(acous.)  12 sec.

Moderate Rock ♩ = 118

*Chord symbols reflect implied harmony.

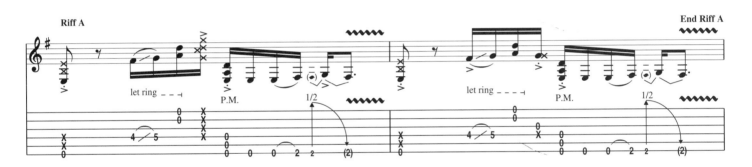

Gtr. 1: w/ Riff A, 2 times, simile

1. I ___ can-not

**Verse**

Gtr. 1: w/ Riff A, 4 times, simile

Em11

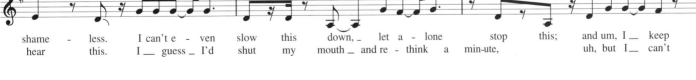

name    this,    I can-not ___ ex- plain    this,    and I real-ly don't    want    to;    a-just call ___ me
an - y sense    I guess ___ I'd    fear    this;    oh, I guess ___ I'd    keep    it    down    so no one ___ would

shame - less.    I can't e - ven    slow    this    down, ___ let a - lone    stop    this;    and um, I ___ keep
hear    this.    I ___ guess I'd    shut    my    mouth ___ and re - think a    min-ute,    uh, but I ___ can't

look - ing ___ a - round ___ but I    can - not    top    this. ___
shut    it    now ___ 'cuz there's some - thing    in it.

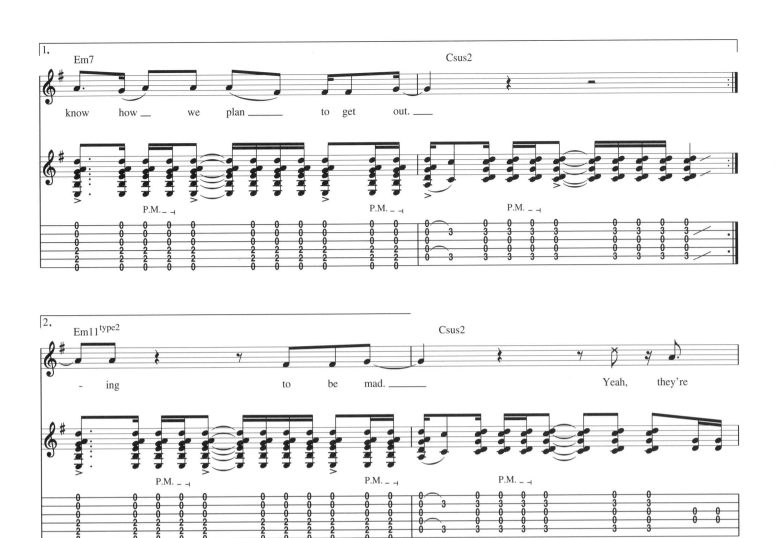

**1.**

know how — we plan — to get out. —

**2.**

-ing to be mad. _____ Yeah, they're

*To Coda* ⊕

go - ing to be mad _____ at us.

**Interlude**
Gtr. 1: w/ Riff A, 2 times, simile

Em11

3. Uh, this is _____ my

**Verse**
Gtr. 1: w/ Riff A, 4 times, 1st time, simile
Gtr. 1: w/ Riff A, 3 times, 2nd time, simile

Em11

skel - e - ton, uh, this is _____ the skin it's _____ in. Uh, that is, _____ ac-
skel - e - ton, uh, give me _____ the skin it's _____ in. Yeah, ba - by,

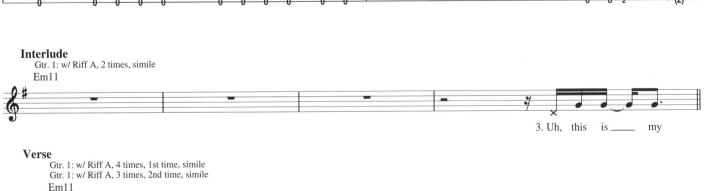

cord - ing to light and grav - i - ty. I'll ___ take off
this is you ac - cord - ing to me. And I nev - er a -

my dis - guise, ___ the mask ___ you met me in, uh, 'cuz I ___ got
vert my eyes, I nev - er com - pro - mise, so nev - er,

some - thing for, for you to see. 4. Just gim-me your
nev - er mind the po - e - try.

*D.S. al Coda*
*(take repeat)*
Gtr. 1: w/ Riff B

⊕ *Coda*

Gtr. 1: w/ Riff A, 1 1/2 times, simile

Em11        Gtr. 1                              A        Em7/A

let ring         P.M.        *mp*        let ring

A        C/G        A        Em7/A        A        C/G

I got-ta cov-er my

Rhy. Fig. 1                                        End Rhy. Fig. 1

let ring        let ring

**Bridge**
Gtr. 1: w/ Rhy. Fig. 1, 5 times, simile
A                Em7/A                A                C/G

butt        'cuz I        cov - et        an - oth - er        man's ___        wife. ___        I got - ta        di - vide ___

A                Em7/A                A                C/G

___ my        e - mo - tions                into        wrong ___ and        right. ___        Then I        get

A                Em7/A                A                C/G

to see how close        I        can        get        to        it        with - out        giv - ing in, ___        and then I        get to

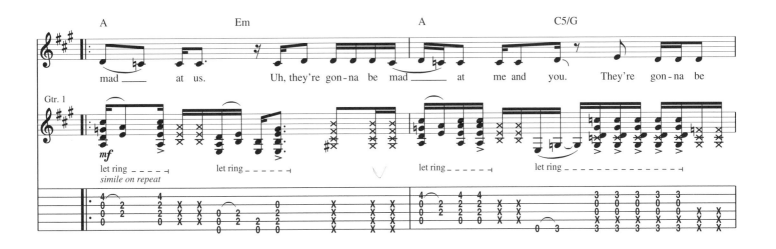

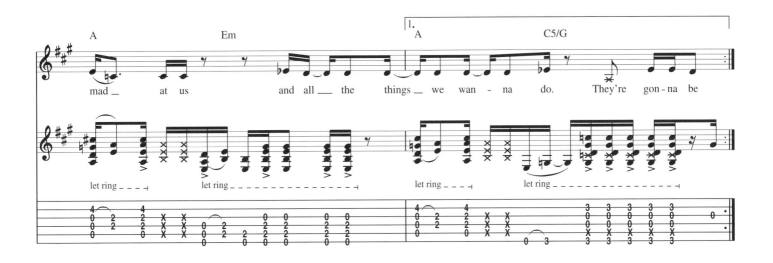

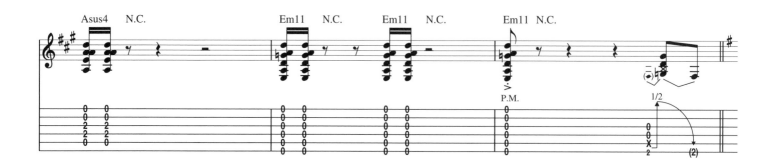

**Interlude**
Gtr. 1: w/ Riff A, 2 times, simile

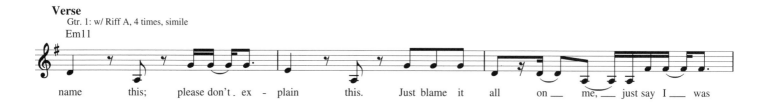

5. Just please don't

**Verse**
Gtr. 1: w/ Riff A, 4 times, simile

name    this;    please don't . ex - plain    this.    Just blame it    all    on __ me, __ just say I __ was

shame    -    less.    Say I could-n't    slow    it    down, __ let a - lone

stop    it;    and say you __ just hung a - round __ 'cuz you could-n't    top    it.

**Outro**
Gtr. 1: w/ Riff A, 1 1/2 times, simile

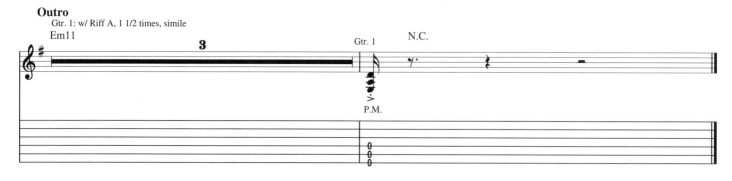

the heat is so great    it plays tricks with the eye    turns the road into water

then from water to sky    there's a crack in the concrete floor

that starts at the sink    there's a bathroom in a gas station    and i've locked myself in it to think

back in the city

the sun bakes the trash on the curb

the men are pissing in doorways

and the rats are running in herds

i got a dream with your face in it    that scares me awake

i put too much on the table    now i got too much at stake

i might let you off easy    i might lead you on    i might wait for you to look for me    and then i might be gone

there's where i come from and    where i'm going

and i am lost in between    i might go out to that phone booth

and leave a veiled invitation    on your machine

you'll stop me won't you    if you've heard this one before    the one where i surprise

you    by showing up at your front door

saying let's not ask what next    or how or why    i am leaving in the morning    so let's not be shy

the door opens

the room winces

the housekeeper comes in    without a warning

i squint at the muscular motel light    and say, hey, good morning    as she jumps her keys jingle

and she leaves as quickly    as she came in    i roll over and taste the pillow with my grin

the sheets are twisted and damp    the heat is so great

and i swear i can feel the mattress    sinking underneath your weight

sleep is like a fever    and i'm glad when it ends    the road flows like a river    it pulls me around every bend

stop me won't you    if you've heard this one before    the one where i surprise you

by showing up at your front door    saying let's not ask what's next

or how or why

i'm leaving in the morning

let's not be shy

SHY

from *Not a Pretty Girl*

# SHY

**Words and Music by Ani DiFranco**

*Symbols in parentheses represent chord names (implied tonality) respective to capoed guitar.
Symbols above reflect actual sounding chords. Capoed fret is "0" in tab.

Gtr. 1: w/ Rhy. Fig. 1, 2 times, simile

shy. _____ 4. The door o -

**Verse**

Gtr. 1: w/ Rhy. Fig. 1, 4 times, simile

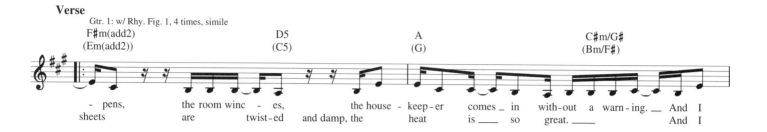

- pens, the room winc - es, the house - keep - er comes _ in with-out a warn - ing. _ And I
sheets are twist - ed and damp, the heat is __ so great. ___ And I

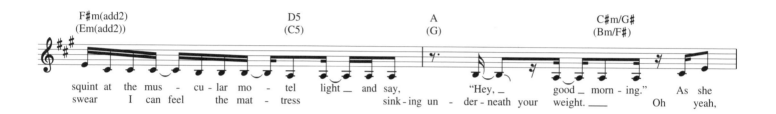

squint at the mus - cu - lar mo - tel light _ and say, "Hey, _ good _ morn - ing." As she
swear I can feel the mat - tress sink - ing un - der - neath your weight. ___ Oh yeah,

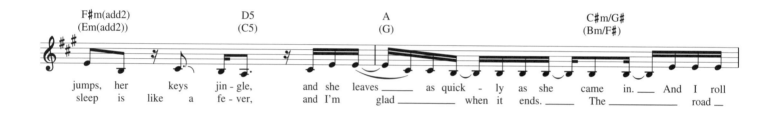

jumps, her keys jin - gle, and she leaves _____ as quick - ly as she came in. _ And I roll
sleep is like a fe - ver, and I'm glad ____ when it ends. ___ The _____ road _

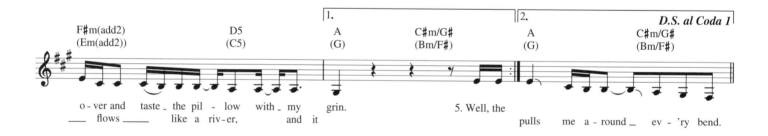

o - ver and taste _ the pil - low with _ my grin. 5. Well, the
___ flows ___ like a riv - er, and it pulls me a - round _ ev - 'ry bend.

**Coda 1**

*D.S.S. al Coda 2*
*(take 3rd ending)*

Gtr. 1: w/ Rhy. Fig. 1, 2 times, simile

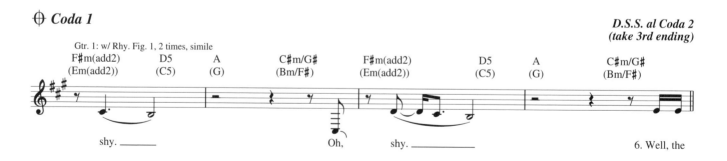

shy. _____ Oh, shy. _____ 6. Well, the

**Coda 2**

Gtr. 1: w/ Rhy. Fig. 2, 4 times

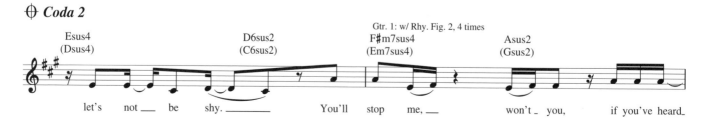

let's not _ be shy. _____ You'll stop me, _ won't _ you, if you've heard_

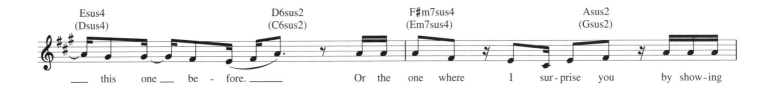

this one be-fore. _____ Or the one where I sur-prise you by show-ing

up at your ___ front ___ door _____ say-ing let's not ask what next, or

how _____ or why. _____ I am leav - ing in the morn - ing, so

Gtr. 1: w/ Rhy. Fig. 3    Gtr. 1: w/ Rhy. Fig. 1, 6 times, simile

let's not ___ be shy, _____ uh, be shy,

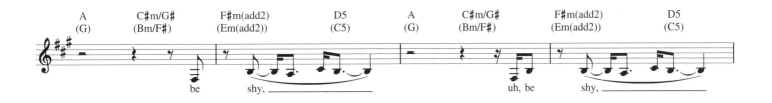

be shy, _____ uh, be shy, _____

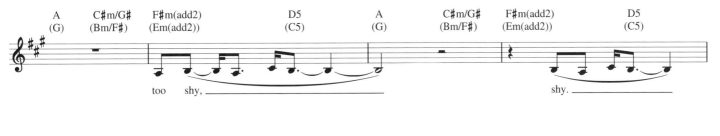

too shy, _____ shy. _____

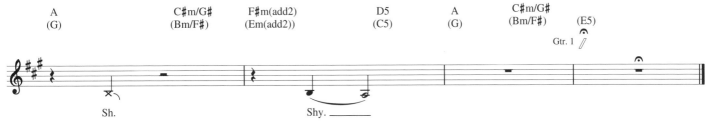

Sh.    Shy. _____

# SoRRY i AM

i'm sorry i didn't sound more excited on the phone
i'm sorry that after all these years
i've left you feeling unrequited and alone
brought you to tears

i guess i never loved you quite as well
as the way you loved me
i guess i'll never really be able to tell you
how sorry i am

i don't know what it is about you
i just know it's not what it was
i don't know why red fades before blue

it just does

and i don't know what it is about me
that i just can't keep still
i keep thinking some day
i will make this all up to you
and maybe some day i will

i guess i never loved you quite as well
as the way you loved me
i guess i'll never really be able to tell you
how sorry i am

from *Not a Pretty Girl*

# SORRY I AM

**Words and Music by Ani DiFranco**

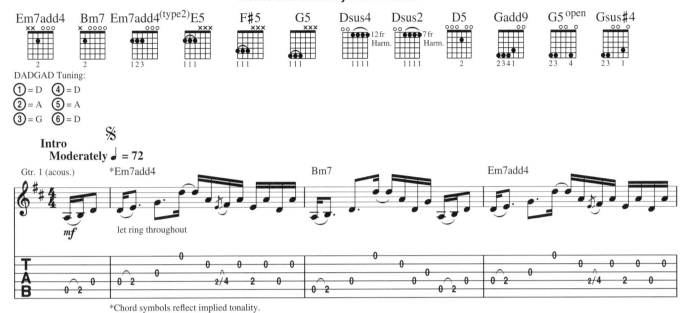

*Chord symbols reflect implied tonality.

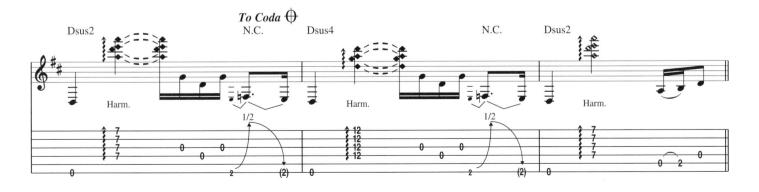

**Verse**

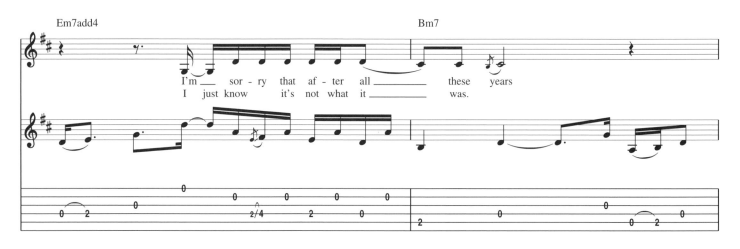

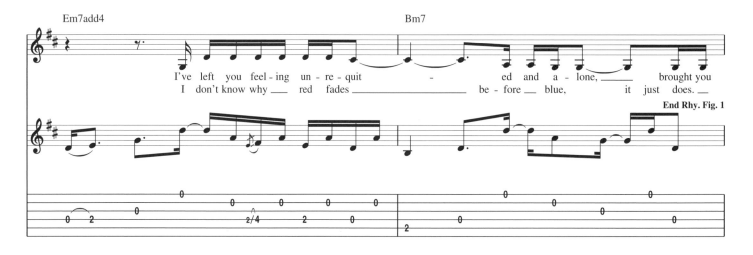

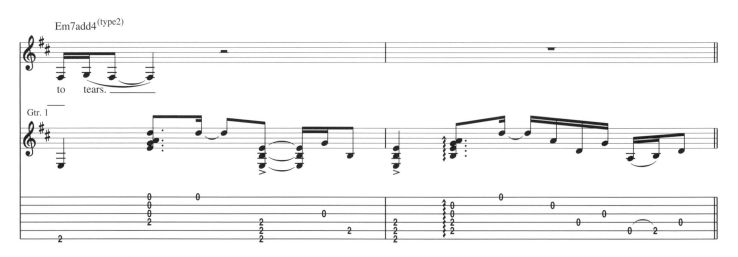

# TALK TO ME NOW

he said ani, you've gotten tough
because my tone was curt
yeah, and when i'm approached in a dark alley
i don't lift my skirt
in this city
self preservation
is a full-time occupation
i'm determined to survive on this shore
i don't avert my eyes anymore
in a man's world i am
a woman by birth
and after nineteen times around i have found
they will stop at nothing
once they know what you are worth
talk to me now
i played the powerless
in too many dark scenes
and i was blessed with a birth and a death
and i guess i just want some say in between
don't you understand
in the day to day
in the face to face
i have to act as strong as i can
just to preserve a place
where i can be who i am
so if you still know how
you can talk to me now

from *Ani DiFranco*
# TALK TO ME NOW
**Words and Music by Ani DiFranco**

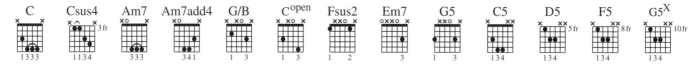

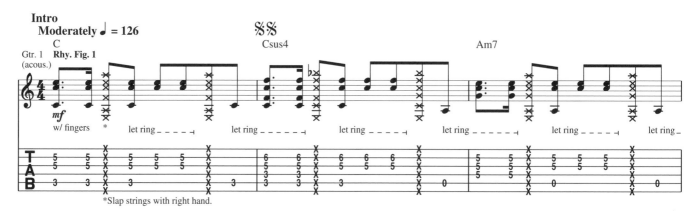

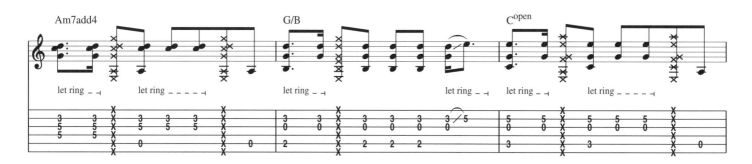

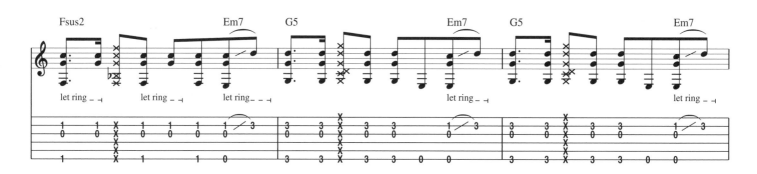

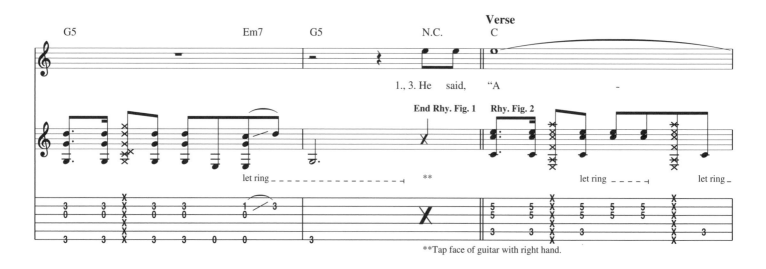

*Slap strings with right hand.

**Tap face of guitar with right hand.

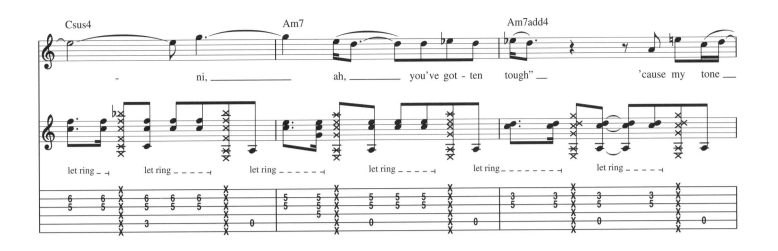

-ni, _____ ah, _____ you've got-ten tough" ___ 'cause my tone ___

was curt. Yeah, and when I'm ___ ap-proached _ in a dark al-ley,

**End Rhy. Fig. 2**

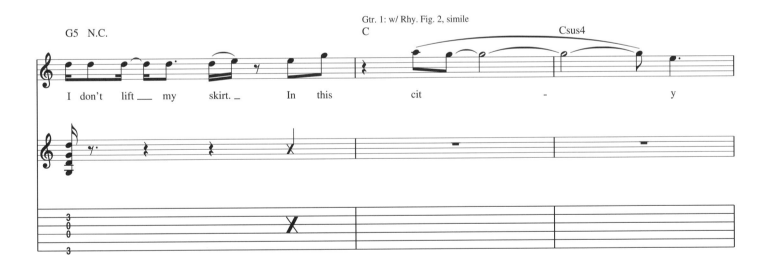

I don't lift ___ my skirt. ___ In this cit - y

Gtr. 1: w/ Rhy. Fig. 2, simile

self - pres - er - va - tion is a full - time _ oc - cu - pa - tion. I'm de - ter - mined to ___ sur -

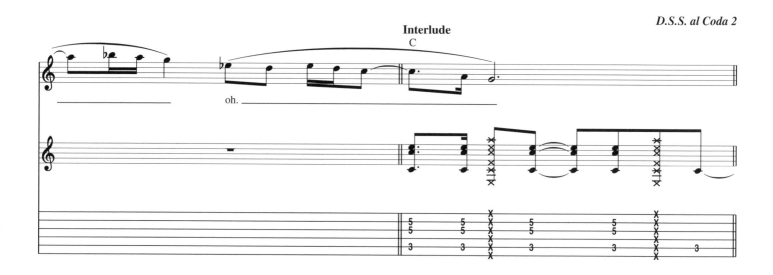

*D.S.S. al Coda 2*

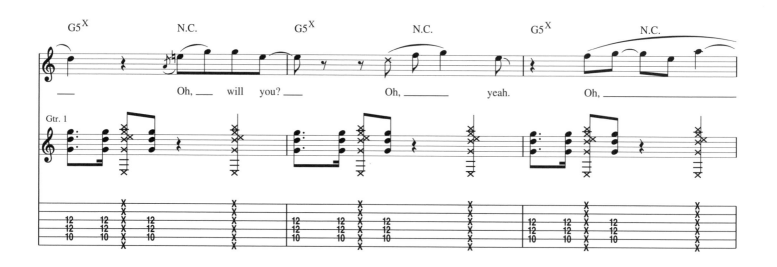

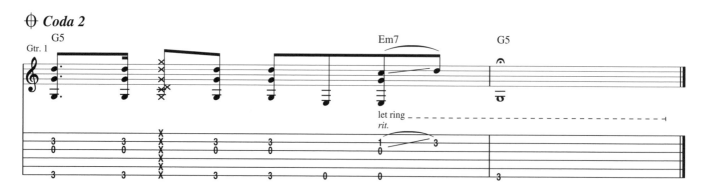

if my life were a movie
there would be a sunset
and the camera would pan away
but the sky is just a little sister
tagging along behind the buildings
trying to imitate their grey
the little boys are breaking bottles
against the sidewalk
the big boys too
the girls are hanging out at the candy store
pumping quarters into the phone
because they don't want to go home

i think what
what if no one's watching
what if when we're dead
we are just dead
i mean what
what if god ain't looking down
what if he's looking up instead

if my life were a movie
i would light a cigarette
and the smoke would curl
around my face
everything i do would be interesting
i'd play the good guy
in every scene
but i always feel i have to
take a stand
and there's always someone on hand
to hate me for standing there
i always feel i have to open my mouth
and every time i do
i offend someone somewhere

but what
what if no one's watching
what if when we're dead
we are just dead
what if there's no time to lose
what if there's things we gotta do
things that need to be said

you know i can't apologize
for everything i know
i mean you don't have to agree with me
but once you get me going
you better just let me go
we have to be able to criticize
what we love
to say what we have to say
'cause if you're not trying
to make something better
then as far as i'm concerned
you are just in the way

i mean what
what if no one's watching
what if when we're dead
we are just dead
i mean what
what if it's just down here
what if god is just an idea
someone put in your head

WHAT iF
NO ONE'S WATCHiNG

from *Imperfectly*

# WHAT IF NO ONE'S WATCHING

### Words and Music by Ani DiFranco

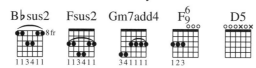

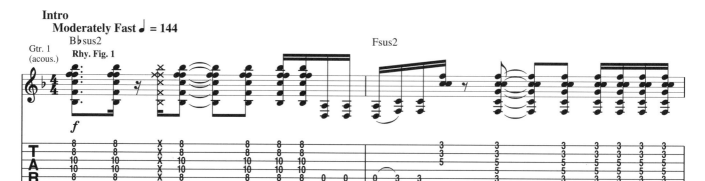

DADGAD Tuning:
① = D   ④ = D
② = A   ⑤ = A
③ = G   ⑥ = D

**Intro**
Moderately Fast ♩ = 144

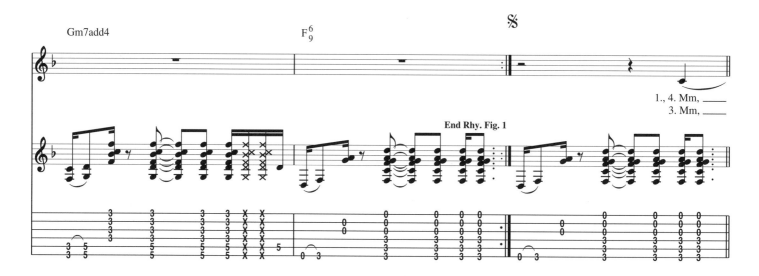

Gtr. 1
(acous.)

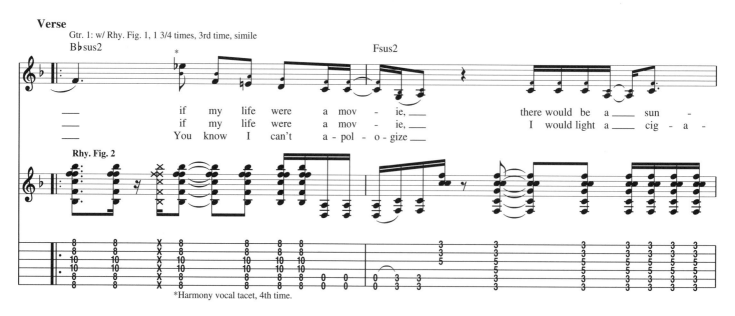

1., 4. Mm, _____
3. Mm, _____

**Verse**
Gtr. 1: w/ Rhy. Fig. 1, 1 3/4 times, 3rd time, simile

_____ if my life were a mov - ie, _____ there would be a _____ sun -
_____ if my life were a mov - ie, _____ I would light a _____ cig - a -
You know I can't a - pol - o - gize

*Harmony vocal tacet, 4th time.

THE WHOLE NIGHT

we can touch
touch our girl cheeks
and we can hold hands
like paper dolls
we can try
try each other on
in the privacy
within new york city's walls
we can kiss
kiss goodnight
and we can go home wondering
what would it be like if
if i did not have a boyfriend
and we could spend
the whole night

i am waking up
in her bed
i sing 1st avenue
the open window said
always late to sleep
late to rise
lying here watching
the day go by
in the living room
there are people on the carpet
having stupid conversations
just to hear themselves talk
and i am drifting through
i am
headed for the kitchen
i am
thinking of her fingers
as i walk

from *Not So Soft*

# THE WHOLE NIGHT

**Words and Music by Ani DiFranco**

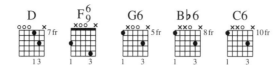

Gtr. 1; DADGAD Tuning:
① = D   ④ = D
② = A   ⑤ = A
③ = G   ⑥ = D

**Intro**
**Moderately** ♩ = 128

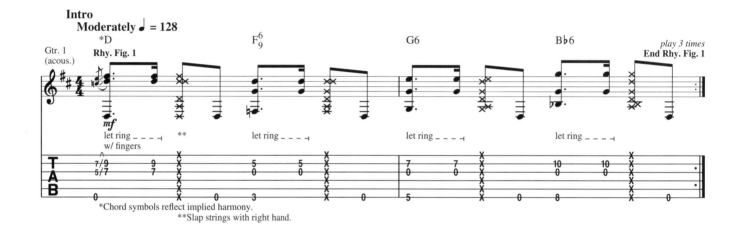

*Chord symbols reflect implied harmony.
**Slap strings with right hand.

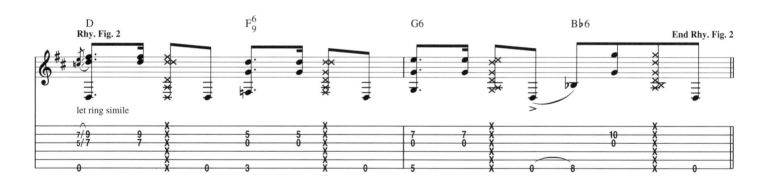

𝄋 **Verse**

Gtr. 1: w/ Rhy. Fig. 2, 3 1/2 times

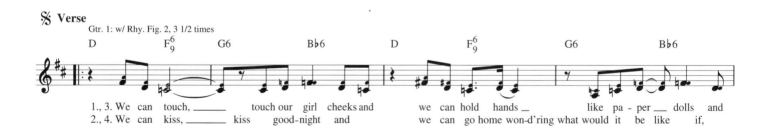

1., 3. We can touch, _____ touch our girl cheeks and     we can hold hands _ like pa-per dolls and
2., 4. We can kiss, _____ kiss good-night and     we can go home won-d'ring what would it be like if,

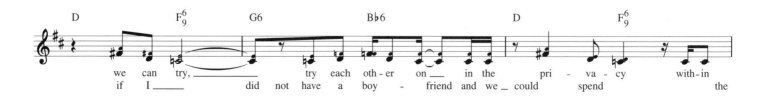

we can try, _____ try each oth-er on _ in the pri-va-cy with-in
if I _____ did not have a boy-friend and we_ could spend the

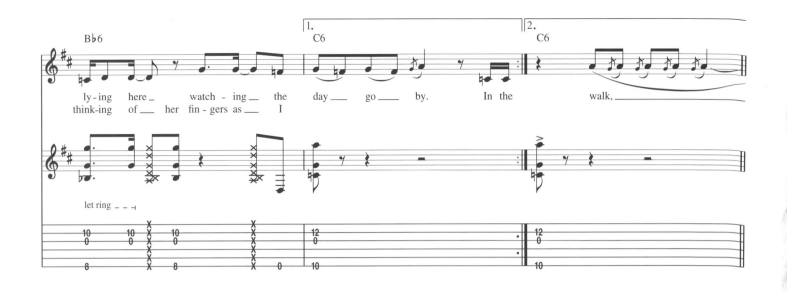

ly - ing    here __    watch - ing __    the    day __    go __    by.    In the                                    walk, __
think-ing    of __    her    fin - gers as __    I

let ring _ _ ⌐

**Interlude**
Gtr. 1: w/ Rhy. Fig. 2, 4 times, simile

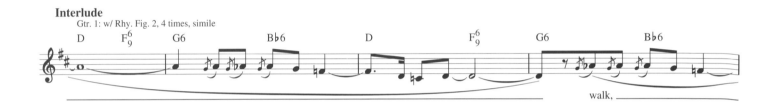

walk, __

*D.S. al Coda*
*(take repeat)*

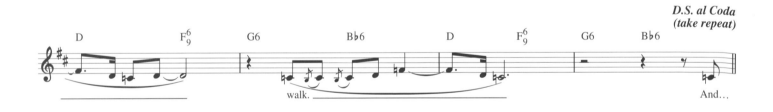

walk.                                                                                              And…

⊕ *Coda*

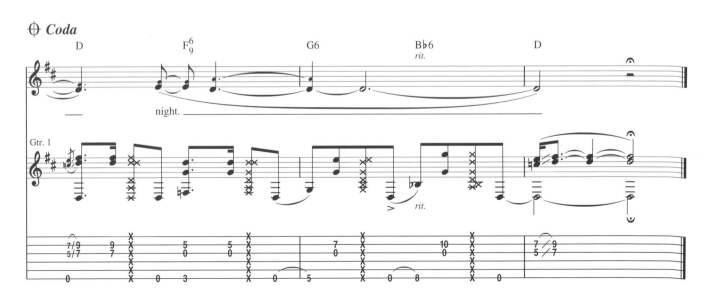

night. __

Gtr. 1